Religious Women
in the
United States

 *Consecrated Life Studies, Volume 4*

Religious Women in the United States

A Survey of the Influential Literature
from 1950 to 1983

by

Elizabeth Kolmer, ASC

Preface by

Marie Augusta Neal, SND de Namur

 Michael Glazier, Inc.

Wilmington, Delaware

About the Author

Elizabeth Kolmer, A.S.C., is Professor of American Studies and History at St. Louis University. She is well respected as a lecturer and scholar. Her publications have appeared in such learned journals as the *Social Justice Review*, *The American Quarterly* and the *Journal of General Education*.

First published in 1984 by Michael Glazier, Inc.
1723 Delaware Avenue, Wilmington, Delaware 19806

©1984 by Michael Glazier, Inc. All rights reserved.

Library of Congress Cataloging in Publication Data

Kolmer, Elizabeth
    Religious women in the United States
    (Consecrated life studies; 4)
    Bibliography: p. 85
    1. Monasticism and religious orders for women—United States—History—
    20th century—Historiography.
    2. Monasticism and religious orders for women—United States—History—
    20th century—Bibliography.
    I. Title.
    II. Series.
    BX4220.U6K65   1984   271'.9'0073   84-81252
    ISBN 0-89453-445-9 (pbk.)

Cover design by Lillian Brulc
Typography by Richard Rein Smith
Printed in the United States of America

DEDICATION

To my parents
Carmelita and Arthur
whose lives of dedication
to God and His people
nurtured
my religious vocation

CONTENTS

ACKNOWLEDGEMENTS

This book began when Dr. Philip Gleason of Notre Dame University asked me to give a paper on "the historiography of religious women since World War II" at the Cushwa Conference on American Catholicism, November 1982. To make the work manageable and focused, I chose to limit the topic to active women's orders in the United States and to deal only with the movement of the renewal of the orders. The response to the paper was heartening, far beyond my expectations, and encouraged me to produce a longer survey which could do greater justice to the topic. I am the first to realize that much more could be said, that many areas of this work could be expanded. I look on this as only a beginning, as a tool for further research that will enable us to better understand where we have been and at what point we are now. Only then can we move into the future to meet the challenges of new directions in religious life.

I wish to thank a number of people who helped along the way. First, I am grateful to Sister Marie Augusta Neal, S.N.D. of Emmanuel College, Boston, Massachusetts, for her encouragement and her willingness to critique the manuscript. Before I began this project I knew her only in name through her publications. Because of this project I came to know her as the intelligent, insightful and charming woman that she is. I am deeply grateful for her prefatory essay to the work.

Thanks also to Sr. Mary Pauline Grady, A.S.C. who read the manuscript for style.

St. Louis University provided the sabbatical time during which I completed the manuscript. A Beaumont Faculty Development Grant from the University's Office of Research Administration facilitated the work of organizing the bibliography. I thank those responsible for this invaluable assistance.

Finally a special thanks to members of my religious community, particularly those at De Mattias Hall, St. Louis, Missouri, who responded to my work with enthusiasm. Together we had experienced the post-Vatican changes of our congregation, the Adorers of the Blood of Christ. Together we also enjoyed recollections of that past through discussion of this project. I am truly grateful for the life we share together and for the support I received from my sisters in this endeavor.

E.K.

PREFACE

Elizabeth Kolmer has done here what anyone who is researching Catholic sisterhoods needs immediately: a chronological review of the literature. Everyone agrees that there have been radical changes in religious congregations of Catholic nuns and sisters, but few know how they began and why. Few looking at the same literature would even agree on what the causes of the changes are, but fewer still are aware of the growing literature documenting the changes or of when the literature began to grow.

No matter what the research thesis to be developed, gathering and reviewing this evidence is essential. Nineteen fifty was a landmark year because, for reasons history records, Pope Pius XII decided to call an international meeting of heads of congregations of men and of women to come to Rome to begin a renewal of religious life. Never before had they gathered, so certainly never before had they deliberated together on what should be done. Like Pope John Paul II, Pope Pius XII had his own ideas on what needed updating and why. Mainly he was concerned with the theological education and professional credentials for those teaching and doing other professional work, but even that emphasis was not new, for it had already begun in 1927 with the publication of Pius XI's encyclical on Catholic education. Pius XII was seeking more. He felt that religious women needed sound theological grounding and the elimination of outdated customs and clothing that estranged them from those they served and rendered their mission less meaningful to the youth of the world. He was concerned about the decline in numbers of young people entering religious congregations in Europe at mid-century.

My data on the changing structures of American Catholic sisterhoods demonstrate that the increase in leavings began in the early fifties, the decrease in the enterings in 1966. All kinds of theses suggest why this was so, but they all need to be tested with fuller knowledge of how the situation was assessed at that time and what directions were set in those years before, during, and after the second Vatican Council. We need to know who was doing the assessment and for whom. By examining the literature by period and by category, Kolmer has done a great service for the researcher and, at the same time, provided the general reader with a most interesting commentary set against major historical events occurring in the same period of history.

One of the highlights in the collection is the description of several group initiatives. (1) The Vatican: A series of Vatican decrees are documented chronologically enabling the reader to see the constant and growing concern of Rome with the contemplative nuns, the teaching sisters, the formation programs, the meaning of the vows, the direction of renewal, and the canons of religious life. (2) National responses: Centers of spirituality were designated in various countries. It was Notre Dame University in the United States, and out of this center came a considerable body of literature advising major superiors and formation personnel how to prepare sisters for religious life; defining what constitutes religious life; directing the spiritual life of religious and, in these directions, defining what constitutes "true" womanhood, "true" spirituality, and "true" conformity to the vowed life. (3) The initiatives of sisters themselves: the foundation and development of the Sister Formation Movement and the Conferences of Major Superiors of Women (CMSW) and of Men (CMSM). Those encouraged and fostered by Rome took on the style and direction of their leaders. Later the founding of the National Association of Women Religious (NAWR), now the National Association of Religious Women (NARW), has a story of its own as a grass-roots action. So too the National Coalition of American Nuns (NCAN) and the sisters' NETWORK. When the CMSW becomes the Leadership Conference of Women Religious (LCWR), the story becomes more contemporary. (4) Finally, the story of each congregation as it met in assembly and revised its constitutions, an action repeated over five hundred times, a massive action that is just hinted at here. All of these events are developed chronologically by Kolmer.

Other highlights include the fact that almost all of the literature written prior to the Second Vatican Council was done by men, except for that provided by the Sister Formation Movement. This transition to women writing for women increases after the Council but does not become a dominant trend until the eighties. To have the literature organized for review and comparison just on this one topic is an historical treasure. Another interesting trend of religious life centers around the treatment of the vows. Here the Council is a transition point, but again the chronological placement of the literature enables one to test the thesis of whether or not the changing emphasis in the mission of the church has a significant effect on the interpretation of the vows. It does, but the exciting thing is to examine the literature with its periodic transitions. Lifestyles made sacred in the context of time and place is the theme most evident to the outside observer. What that observer lacks that this literature supplies are the rationales for the transitions.

Essential elements, commitment, secularization, mission, apostolic spirituality, and cloister all have their place. The main focus is literature written by church people for church people. Kolmer's intent is to report on the literature that describes religious life in the United States between 1950 and 1983. She does just this in the voices of those writing during this period. Granted, some voices are heard more clearly than others; that emphasis is itself part of the richness of the report. It is an account to stimulate other accounts. It is the kind of gift that only an historian can provide, that controlled intent to let time determine the order of treatment and what story will be told. Let the sociologist read in terms of definition of the situation, the psychologist focus on personality development, the theologian be surprised in her search for where God is, and the ethicist examine the shifting social and personal concerns. What the historian has done is let us know what can be found today in library and archives.

The account challenges the archivist to fill in the blanks with those accumulated documents each congregation is storing. All of those who assumed that the story began later must reexamine assumptions about causes, and those who think nothing really changed can now come and see what wonders have been wrought, see what was said then and what is happening now. Catholic women in congregations today, alive with the mission of the church and filled with hope in the application of their spirit and commitment to the new needs of the world today for life in the church, are facing formidable obstacles to growth and development with imagination, caring, and faith. This monograph recounts that trend, suggests its diversity and the influences guiding it. It is indeed a useful tool for analysis, planning and understanding.

Marie Augusta Neal, SND

INTRODUCTION

As the decade of the fifties opened, the people of the United States hoped for a more stable world now that the turbulence of a World War was safely past. There was still the presence of Communism that lurked as an ever-present threat to a unified world. Nonetheless, the Eisenhower era was perceived as a time of peace and relative stability. Few realized the coming effect of the 1954 Supreme Court case which ended segregation, or the long-range results of sending advisers to Vietnam in mid-decade, or even of the launching of Sputnik in 1957. By decade's end some Americans were concerned over the challenges to the system revealed in the Montgomery bus boycott of 1956 and knew that the tensions shown in the integration of Central High School in Little Rock, Arkansas, the following year were only signs of things to come.

It was a time of greater change than most realized. For the moment, however, it was a time of sprawling suburbia, of middle-of-the-road politics supported by a growing economic and social middle class whose first concern was upward mobility undergirded by family and home. The Catholic Church in the 1950's stood solid and reasonably self-assured of its identity and its place in American society. It experienced a phenomenal growth in membership from less than 28 million in 1950 to more than 43 million in 1963.

Bishop Fulton Sheen kept the Church before the American public with his magnetic television presentations and his inspirational publications on practical aids to Christian living. Fulton Oursler's book on the Gospels remained popular, as did Thomas Merton's much published story of conversion to Catholicism and his vocation to the Trappist life.

Catholic institutions abounded and increased — churches, hospitals, parochial schools, diocesan high schools, and four year colleges. Catholic parents, like other Americans, tried to give their children a better education on each level than they themselves had received. School and parish complemented the American Catholic's primary interest of home and family. The mainstay of many of these institutions, especially the hospitals and schools, was the members of religious orders, particularly religious women, who for many years staffed these institutions for a nominal stipend. In 1950 Catholic religious women numbered 147,000 with promise of increase as each year young women responded to the call of the Church. By 1963 at the opening of Vatican Council II they numbered 177,154.

After the war American women had returned to their homes to bear, raise, and nurture the nation's families. A life dedicated to the work of the Church opened many opportunities to a young Catholic woman in a day when the single career woman was not yet socially accepted. The life of religious women (even those women devoted to such apostolic works as teaching and nursing which took them daily into the workaday world) was essentially separated from the flow of secular life. Garbed in long robes and intricate headpieces of infinite variations, they lived highly regulated lives according to the discipline of rules and traditional conventual practice. They were a group set apart, highly respected in Catholic parish and diocese and in non-Catholic circles as well. The call to the religious state, or to be a nun, was a respected way of life for the young Catholic woman.

It was in these years, however, that changes in religious orders began to occur, not perceptible to the general public, or in some cases even to many of the members of the orders. It was a movement for gradual change initiated primarily by the Sacred Congregation for Religious in Rome in discussions with the major superiors of the orders. The suggested changes included a renewal of religious spirit and an adaptation of conventual practice. Publications from Pius XII and especially from the Sacred Congregation showed a concern that these changes be effected with proper regard for authority and obedience and that in all these changes unanimity and peace of mind among all religious prevail. (Larroana to Mothers General, *Review for Religious*, 1954, 297). The directives from Rome, both from the Pope and from the Sacred Congregation in this pre-Vatican era are numerous and in most cases very pointed on the areas of religious life to be changed or adapted. Interpretation of the necessity and urgency of these changes for individual orders was left to the superiors so that involvement of most religious in the ranks was minimal. In the early sixties, with a changing social climate and the pronouncements of Vatican Council II, the base of participation in the process of renewal broadened and hastened the process considerably.

The history of change in women's religious orders of the Catholic Church in the recent past is a phenomenon which merits the attention of the serious historian. The sources for such a study are voluminous, both for the study of individual congregations and for research on the movement as a whole. This essay attempts to present a survey of the literature published in English from 1950 to 1983 dealing with the renewal of women religious in the active apostolic orders. A bibliography is attached for reference and as an aid to further research.

Chapter One

PRE-VATICAN II

Millions of pilgrims flocked to Rome in 1950 to honor the proclamation of the Holy Year and to fulfill the required devotions for the indulgences of the year of jubilee. Among them was a group who, without a doubt, observed the pious practice of gaining the Holy Year indulgences. Their reason for coming, however, was otherwise. This group of men and women major superiors, representative of the contemplative and monastic religious orders of the world, had been called to Rome by the Sacred Congregation of Religious for the first General Assembly of Religious. The meeting, held November 26 to December 8, was of historic importance; never had there been a convocation like this in the history of the Church. The message of the meeting was equally noteworthy: the renewal and adaptation of religious life. Pius XII, in a letter to Cardinal Micara, Prefect of the Congregation for Religious, commended him for the convocation. In his letter the Pontiff noted the need for adaptation of religious life lest "the holy laws of each Institute degenerate into an assemblage of exterior regulations uselessly imposed, whose letter, in the absence of the spirit, kills." (*The States of Perfection*, St. Paul's Editions, 1967).

Participants at the assembly received the Pontiff's Apostolic Constitution *Sponsa Christi* (November 21, 1950), in which Pius XII noted the "excessively strict interpretation of enclosure." He recognized the necessity for certain accessory practices essential to the spirit of an order but noted: "We find some other things in the institutes of nuns which are neither necessary or complimentary; they are merely extrinsic and historical. And so we have decreed . . . to introduce cautiously and prudently those adaptations to present-day conditions which will be able to bring not only greater dignity but also greater efficacy to this institute." He concluded the document with general norms to accomplish this adaptation.

In his address closing this first international congress, the Pope spoke again of the limits, methods and program for this renewal, and asked religious institutes "to adapt themselves to changed times and to combine the old and the new in a happy alliance." Proceedings of this assembly, published in Latin, filled four large volumes. In 1962 Vitus Gaiani published an abbreviated version, *For a Better Religious Life* (Alba House, St. Paul). His book is a synthesis of the basic ideas of the assembly rather than a report of the proceedings as such. From a vast amount of material, Gaiani presented the Assembly's ideas on the ascetical and theological aspects of religious life, especially on the vows and common life. The final section on adaptation of religious life discussed the necessity to distinguish between essentials and non-essentials of religious orders. This last chapter reveals a cautious attitude especially in the changes in practices regarding such things as accessibility of newspapers and the use of such modern technology as radio, movies, and the telephone.

Almost immediately Rome planned a subsequent meeting for September, 1951, this one for members of teaching orders. Noting the rising gulf between youth and the sisters in the schools, the Pope called for necessary adaptations which he enumerated specifically: "The religious habit: Select one of such a kind that it will be an expression of interior unaffectedness, of simplicity and religious modesty; then it will serve to edify all, even modern youth." He called the sisters to a greater involvement in the work of the Church and encouraged them to make use of those things necessary for carrying on their work. He asked them to adapt their horarium to the needs of the apostolate and to discard those remnants of a past age which complicated the educational task. He required professional training for the teaching sisters equivalent to, or better than, that of their secular counterparts. The young teaching sister should have a perfect knowledge and command of the subject, receive a good preparation and formation, and meet the qualifications demanded by the State. Parents who send their daughters to the Sisters' schools for Christian upbringing should not have the disadvantage of an inferior education. Rather, they should have guarantee of the best instruction for their daughters. (*States of Perfection*, p. 412).

Almost no year passed in the decade of the fifties without a new directive from the Pontiff for institutes of religious. In his allocution to General Superiors, again called to an international congress in September 1952, noting the vocation crisis that was apparent, especially in European countries, he asked the superiors to conform with his directives "courageously." "In this crisis of vocations," he said, "take care that your customs, the kind of life or the asceticism of your religious families be not a barrier. We are speaking of certain usages which, if they had a meaning in another cultural context, no longer have one today.... The religious habit should express consecration. For the rest, let the habit be suitable and meet the requirements of hygiene. In sum, in non-essentials adapt yourselves as far as reason and well ordered charity make it advisable." (*States of Perfection*, 425).

In March 1954, Pius XII published his encyclical *Sacra Virginitas* in which he extolled the life dedicated to virginity, refuted certain contemporary errors on the subject, and exhorted church members to foster vocations at this critical time. (*States of Perfection*, 432) Reiterating the need for professional competence of young religious, the Pontiff approved Regina Mundi in Rome as a pontifical institute of

higher learning (1956) "for training, education and formation of religious women in the sciences and disciplines."
(*States of Perfection*, 472)

Besides a second general congress of religious superiors in
1957, the Sacred Congregation held other meetings
throughout the decade with individual orders, national
groups of women religious, men religious, contemplative
orders, and the like. These meetings produced further directives for renewal, much of which was applicable to religious
life generally. These documents are available in the collection of papal documents, *States of Perfection* (1967).

The Congress of 1950 in Rome, attended by some 4000
representatives, was hardly the type of gathering to effect
realistic planning. For this reason the Sacred Congregation
requested that national congresses be held throughout the
world. Religious of the United States held their first congress at Notre Dame University in 1952. Proceedings of the
Sisters' section of the congress were published in *Sisters'
Religious Community Life in the United States* (Paulist
Press, 1952). The papers reflected the earlier requests of the
Sacred Congregation and of the Pope: that religious orders
share information and discuss their common problems; that
there be a concern for the professional and religious formation of the sisters; and that the practices of religious life be
adapted to the modern world. The directives of the Holy See
regarding the professional and religious education of sisters
fell on newly planted ground in the United States. In 1941
Sister Bertrande Meyers, D.C. had published her work on
The Education of Sisters (Sheed and Ward) in which she set
out the historical aspects of the question, a survey of the
current situation, several recommendations, and a proposed plan for a "pre-service program" for young religious.
Another pioneer, Sister Madeleva Wolff, C.S.C. had presented a paper at the National Catholic Educational Association's annual meeting in 1949 on "The Education of Sister
Lucy." At the 1952 meeting of the NCEA a panel on teacher
education discussed Pius XII's "Directives to Teaching
Sisters."

Several sisters who would become prominent in the Sister

Formation movement, among them Sister Mary Emil, I.H.M., Sister Richardine, B.V.M. and Sister Ritamary Bradley, C.H.M., surveyed religious orders in 1952 regarding their formation programs, their plans for the future, and their available facilities for professional formation. The papers of the Sister Formation annual conferences, held through the decade of the fifties, were published under the editorship of Sister Ritamary by Fordham University Press: *The Mind of the Church in the Formation of Sisters* (1956); *The Spiritual and Intellectual Elements in the Formation of Sisters* (1957); *Planning for the Formation of Sisters* (1958) and *The Juniorate in Sister Formation* (1960). From 1954 to 1964 the Sister Formation Conference, as it came to be called, published its official quarterly *Bulletin*, which contained major articles on the preparation and formation of religious teachers, reports and comments from the regional conferences and biographical data for further reading. Fortunately for the historical researcher, a reprint collection of the Sister Formation *Bulletin* is available in three volumes (I, II: Marquette University Press, 1959, 1963; III: St. Paul: North Central Publishing Co., 1965). Noteworthy for the historian in these volumes are Sister Mary Emil's account of the history of the Sister Formation movement (I, reprint: Supplement I); the development of the Sister Formation Marillac College, St. Louis, Missouri (VI, No.3); and notes on the development of the Everett Curriculum (III, No.1). The Everett Curriculum itself was published in complete form in *Report of the Everett Curriculum* (Seattle, 1956) and in summary form as an appendix to Sister Ritamary's *Planning for the Formation of Sisters.*

A list of source material for the study of the Sister Formation movement is not complete without mention of the works of Elio Gambari. His publications are numerous and in some way all are pertinent to the development of religious life since 1950. As a member of the Sacred Congregation of Religious he became an important and welcome resource for the Sister Formation movement. Many of his publications were the result of the numerous lectures he delivered at the Sister Formation summer workshops. Although most of his publications are of a later date, his address on the juniorate (see Sister Ritamary, *The Juniorate in Sister Formation*) and his *Religious Women in Canon Law* (P. Reilly, 1960) are pertinent to this pre-Vatican era.

Sister Formation and the National Congress of Religious at the University of Notre Dame were the first responses to the directives given by the Holy See in 1950. The Sacred Congregation also directed religious leaders to form national associations of religious superiors in order to facilitate the movement of adaptation and renewal. Consequently, at a November, 1956, meeting in Chicago, Illinois, the Conference of Major Superiors of Women was formed. Proceedings and reports of their annual meetings have not been published as systematically as those of the Sister Formation Conference. Research on this organization would have to start with the office of the Leadership Conference of Religious Women, the title under which the major superiors are organized at present. In 1956 the Sister Formation Conference became a department of the Major Superiors at the suggestion of the Sacred Congregation of Religious. (See Sister Formation *Bulletin.* I, reprint, p.237.)

Forward-looking colleges and universities developed programs through the fifties in keeping with the new directions. The best known and most representative was the Institute of Spirituality sponsored by the Theology Department of the University of Notre Dame. In August of each year, the theology faculty gathered widely recognized scholars to provide a one-week in-service program for religious. The topics varied — studies of the vows, the nature of religious government, the formation of novices, psychological problems in religious life, liturgical developments, the apostolate of teaching, sociological aspects of religious authority were some of the topics. *Proceedings* of these institutes were published yearly by the University of Notre Dame Press (ed. Joseph Haley, C.S.C. 1953; 1957-1959; ed. Leonard Collins, C.S.C. 1956-1958). In-service courses of this type were important in the movement for renewal since none of the sisters actively involved in apostolic service had had the benefit of the newly developing formation programs. The courses underscored the need for on-going formation of sisters in the field and acquainted participants with the latest research in religious matters. Selected addresses from these courses were republished in the early sixties by the University of Notre Dame Press in a seven-volume series under the general title *Religious in the Modern World.*

Some of the best discussions on religious life were compiled in a ten-volume series, *Religious and Modern Problems,* first published in Europe and reprinted in this country in the pre-Vatican era (Newman Press). Each volume was a compilation of the writings of prominent theologians on the topic being treated. The first volume, *Religious Sisters,* dealt with the question of renewal as seen from the context of theology of religious life. Other volumes in the series treated of the vows, communal life, apostolate, and vocation. The need for sisters to be professional, competent, and well instructed in matters of religious life received strong emphasis throughout the volumes. (See bibiography, Religious Life Series.)

In August, 1961, twelve hundred religious women met for the Second National Congress of Religious in the United States. The Congress had been suggested by the Sacred Congregation and was sponsored by the Conference of Major Superiors of Women. At this assembly they planned to review their progress, evaluate their response to the appeal of Pius XII for renewal, strengthen the formation programs already begun, and come to a better understanding of the apostolate. Again, it was attended by members of the Sacred Congregation; outstanding scholars from Europe and the United States addressed the assembled religious. One section of the meeting was an appeal to send religious personnel to work in Latin American countries. A survey was taken of communities already involved in Latin America and those who planned to respond to this request in the near future. The meeting was another step towards greater unity of purpose and cooperation among communities which the Pope had asked for eleven years before. Papers and addresses of the meeting were documented in *Religious*

Life in the Church Today published by the University of Notre Dame Press (1961).

But what of the daily life of the nun in its lived reality between 1950 and the beginnings of Vatican II in 1962? The developments in religious life as described above really touched chiefly the religious superiors and the formation personnel who attended the meetings and the institutes. In many communities it affected to some extent the candidates in initial formation programs, especially postulants, novices and young professed. It affected the lives of the sisters in the apostolate only in so far as they were told that there would not be a group of new teachers available until such time as the newly professed sisters had completed their professional training. This caused a strain on the sisters working in the schools because already they had more work than they could handle and now no relief was forthcoming in the immediate future. The life of the rank-and-file sister at this time was one of carrying a heavy load of teaching — frequently in overcrowded classrooms — supervising children, training choirs and altar boys, and caring for church and sacristy. The Catholic schools were staffed by the sisters exclusively. Only as a rare exception did a pastor hire a lay teacher. It was an accepted fact that sisters were the necessary component of the Catholic school. With the increase in population of school-age children in the fifties, there was a constant demand for more sisters to fill newly added classrooms. In that sense there was a shortage of sisters, even while each year there was an increase in their number. Added to the heavy workload of the sisters was a more or less unbending daily schedule — rising at 5 a.m. for common morning prayer and meditation, followed by Mass or a communion service. Traditional schedules of lengthy prayer and common recreation continued throughout this time, an obvious indication that the words of the Pontiff regarding adaptation had a long way to go before anything would happen to change the lives of the sisters. Even though superiors had been exhorted directly by the Pope to make significant changes in religious life, the possibility of this being accomplished was limited by the superior's own conviction or lack of it. Even when she was convinced of such a need, the question still remained, how? Lastly, there was the problem of convincing the rank-and-file sister of the need for adaptation.

Publications of the fifties revealed many facets of the life of religious women in its lived reality. Several books gave descriptive accounts of life in the convent. At times realistic, at times romantic, these books, frequently used as vocation pieces, served as apologia for convent life. They showed the ups and downs of the young woman in process of becoming a nun, attempted to depict religious as real people, and convent life as not so rigid and dull after all. None of them raised the question of changing the traditional practices of the religious life. *And Nora Said Yes* by Sister M. Vianney (1953) and *All the Days of My Life* by Sister M. Jeremy (1959) represent this group well.

It was in the area of the spiritual reading required daily of the sisters that the need for renewal was the most apparent. Many works of this type were superficial discussions of the spiritual life with heavy emphasis on the practice of such virtues as humility, trust, obedience, and modesty. Explanations of the virtues had little, if any, theological content or scriptural base. Authors Hyacinth Blocker (*Good Morning, Good People*, 1954), John Moffatt (*Look, Sister*, 1956 and many others), Winifred Herbst (*The Sisters Are Asking*, 1956), Bruno Hagspiel (*Convent Readings and Reflections*, 1959) and John Murphy (*The Virtues on Parade*, 1959) represent some of the more simplistic discussions of the spiritual life. Better for their times were Robert Gleason (*To Live is Christ*, 1968) and Romano Guardini (*Prayer in Practice*, 1957).

Books for the spiritual nourishment of sisters, often presented as retreat notes or conferences, emphasized obedience as a primary virtue. Authors Felix Duffy (*With Anxious Care*, 1950), Ignaz Waterott (*Guidance for Religious*, 1950), Francis X. Ronsin (*To Govern Is To Love*, 1955), and Ferdinand Valentine (*Religious Obedience*, 1952) treated solely of this pre-eminent virtue. Emphasis was on the duty of the subject to do what she was told, even if she did not understand the need for the order. In most cases they advocated little, if any, representation on the part of the subject. The concept of obedience and authority in the religious community focused only on the superior who commanded and the subject who obeyed. These books were written almost exclusively by male clerics, and even when they were written specifically for women religious, the author utilized the male pronoun throughout as well as the generic "man." Sister Mary Laurence (*The Convent in the Modern World*, 1954; *Nuns Are Real People*, 1955; *One Nun To Another*, 1959) is one of the few exceptions to the male author. Unfortunately her books were generally no more solidly based than theirs.

Several publications from the pre-Vatican II era reflected an earlier new development, the recognition by Rome of the secular institute as a new form of religious life. Members of the secular institutes are dedicated to the work of the Church but do not live the communal life in the same manner as the traditional orders. In 1947 Pope Pius XII had issued his apostolic constitution *Provida Mater Ecclesia* in which he recognized secular institutes as a state of perfection and defined the rules to govern them. Mary Florence O'Leary's *Our Time is Now*, (1956) and Joseph Perinelle's *God's Highways* (1958) both dealt with the secular institute as it derived from the older forms. One senses that these works, although addressed to members of secular institutes and to the religious of traditional orders, had as their primary interest a better understanding and acceptance on the part of the traditional religious. O'Leary particularly explained the reasons why these new religious groups rejected some of the traditional practices of religious life, especially those rules that would limit their apostolic activity.

New editions of works on Canon Law for religious were indicative of changes taking place in religious orders. In 1958 Joseph Cruisen updated his *Religious Men and Women in Church Law*. Kevin O'Rourke's highly readable revision of Louis Fanfani's earlier work *Canon Law for Religious Women* was done in the light of "several important instructions and responses affecting the laws for religious women issued by the Holy See." Elio Gambari's three conferences *Religious Women in Church Law* (1960) published by the Institute of Spirituality in Philadelphia especially pointed out the need for adaptation.

In 1959 Rene Carpentier published *Life in the City of God*, a complete revision of the *Catechism of the Vows* which for many years had served as an introduction to the religious life. Carpentier's work was based on Scripture, church teaching, and canon law and became a welcome replacement for the older text used for initial formation. Foreshadowing concepts from Vatican II, the author commented in the introduction that "at all costs we must avoid any idea of personal superiority on the part of religious." In contrast to the older *Catechism*, Carpentier presented the three religious vows, not as three grave obligations, but as a "whole of life under the influence of love which appeals for the unreserved gift of self."

Gerald Kelly's *Guidance for Religious* (1956) dealing with spiritual direction for sisters was also an indication of later developments. The author took into account the whole person, not just her religious and spiritual life. Noteworthy was his inclusion of a section on emotional maturity. In a brief comment on obedience he emphasized availability rather than the traditional interpretation of simply doing what one was told by legitimate authority. The subject of the last chapter, "What to Do about the Race Problem," revealed Kelly's broader vision. Few works at this time raised social questions as important for religious. Here Kelly called the Christian, and more so the religious, to recognize the human dignity of blacks. He noted the type of segregated and humiliated life that blacks were forced to live, even separated in places of worship. He gave directives on behavior of the religious in word and act and enjoined them to examine their attitude towards black members of society.

Reflected in the pre-Vatican II literature was a growing concern for the number and quality of vocations. Pius XII had noted the decline in vocations, especially in Europe, when he addressed the first International Congress of Religious in 1950. Beginning in 1947 and through the decade of the fifties, the University of Notre Dame held an annual vocation institute. Perusal of the proceedings makes one aware that these institutes did not have the depth that the Institute on Spirituality had. In December 1961, the first International Congress on Vocations convened in Rome. In his address, John XXIII extolled the religious vocation, noted the limitless forms of dedication to Christ, and encouraged those involved in vocation work to use all modern means — the press, the radio, and television — in their recruiting. Proceedings of this congress, published in *Today's Vocation Crisis* (1962), gave evidence of greater involvement of social scientists in research on religious life. The translators-editors — Godfrey Poage and Germain Lievin — included a lengthy bibliography of publications on vocation between 1920 and 1960.

Several social scientists pioneered in applying their disciplines to the study of religious life. Joseph Fichter taught courses on sociology of vocation at the University of Notre Dame beginning in 1955 and participated in the Institute of Spirituality for Sisters in 1959. His publication *Religion as an Occupation* (1961) was an outgrowth of the research for these lectures. In it he discussed vocation in its relation to society and the sociological aspects of leaving the religious vocation.

Discussion on screening candidates to religious life by means of psychological testing existed as early as the 1930's and 1940's. The Notre Dame Vocation Institute had discussed the topic in 1954, as had the National Catholic Educational Association. William Bier, who published his work on seminarians and the use of the Minnesota Multiphasic Personality Test in 1948, discussed testing procedures and their value at the 1959 Notre Dame Institute of Spirituality. In *Screening for the Priesthood or Religious Life* (1962) Magda Arnold and co-authors discussed types and uses of testing. The book was technical in its use of terminology and results and included valuable bibliographical data for those interested in further research. Less professionally technical was Trafford Maher's *Lest We Build on Sand* (1962), which discussed the natural basis for religious life.

Periodical Literature

Of the many religious periodicals on the market before Vatican II, the most pertinent for the study of renewal in religious life is the *Review for Religious*. This journal followed very closely the movement for adaptation and discussed the topic in a straightforward manner. Many of its articles in the fifties dealt with the devotional/spiritual life of religious, in much the same way as other journals did. However, side by side with such articles the *Review* published the directives of the Pope and the Sacred Congregation.

Explanatory articles on the Roman documents kept the directives from Rome in the minds of religious. There was a noticeable increase in such articles as the sixties opened and preparations for the Council were underway.

A number of articles in the pre-Vatican *Review* are noteworthy for the historian of religious renewal. In September 1952 the *Review* published an account of the first national Congress of Religious at Notre Dame. The article is a summary of the salient points of the papers and a full list of papers delivered. Though all too brief, this is one of the few readily available accounts of this important event.

It is noteworthy in discussions of the three vows that the *Review* gave greatest attention to the vow of obedience if one can judge by quantity of articles published. The emphasis in the articles on obedience remained for the most part on the duty of the subject to fulfill the orders of the superior. A good bit of comment centered on the notion of "obedience of the judgment" and "intellectual obedience" — how the subject might reconcile a difference of judgment with the superior regarding the command given. Although the judgment of the superior was generally given the priority in the articles, there was present a growing consideration of the subject's views and her integrity as a mature adult. Articles by Thomas Dubay ("Superior's Precept and Will of God," November, 1961; "Personal Integrity and Intellectual Obedience," September, 1963) and Sister Teresa Mary ("Religious Obedience and Critical Thinking," September, 1963), among others, revealed the theological perspectives prevalent at that time. The psychological ramifications of obedience were discussed by Thomas Dubay ("The Psychological Possibility of Intellectual Obedience," January, 1960) and by psychologist Richard Vaughan ("Obedience and Psychological Maturity," September, 1962). Other articles dealt with the nature of authority, role of superiors and role of subjects. The coming broader interpretations of obedience can be seen in J. Tillard ("Religious Obedience, Mystery of Communion," January, 1965) and Thomas Dubay ("Renewal in Exercise of Authority," November, 1965). Both of these authors emphasize the need for dialogue between the sisters of the community and the superior.

Other than an occasional article on modesty, the *Review* carried no article on the vow of chastity before 1961. Later articles between 1961 and 1965 showed the influence of the Council's deliberations in so far as the interpretation of chastity presented sexual love as a good the renunciation of which should lead to a life of total love. The authors' efforts to place their discussions in the context of Scripture and the tradition of the Church resulted in some of the first attempts to develop a theology of this vow for general readership among religious. Lucien LeGrand ("Prophetical Meaning of Chastity," September, 1961; "Spiritual Value of Virginity According to St. Paul," May, 1963) and Charles Schleck ("Sanctification Through Virginity," November, 1965) are representative. The psychosexual development of the celibate person was discussed by Richard Vaughan ("Chastity and Psychosexual Development," November, 1964) and Richard McCormick ("Psychosexual Development in Religious Life," November, 1964).

The vow of poverty received the least attention in the *Review* during the pre-Vatican II era. Though Edward

Garesche published "Spirit of Poverty and Modern Times" as early as January 1950, no further article continued the discussion throughout the decade. When in September 1962 Andre Auw published "Contentment: Child of Poverty," there was a change in the approach to the vow. Garesche, reflecting the traditional approach to the vows prior to the Council, distinguished between the vow and the virtue of poverty, giving emphasis to the ownership and disposition of material goods as stated in Canon Law for Religious. Later articles by Auw, by Paul Bernidicou ("Religious Poverty and the Modern Age," November, 1964) and Charles Schleck ("Poverty and Sanctification," July, 1965) were more pastoral, dwelling on the spirit of poverty (Bernidicou says "The soul of poverty is charity," p. 775), the attitudes and the responsibilities of the individual religious.

Prior to the Council, the work of religious in general centered, almost exclusively, in parishes, hospitals or other institutions where they served. Living arrangements were nearby; all religious who worked in the institution lived together. In many respects, development of community life was discussed very little by religious or their superiors except in the context of urging members to peaceful and harmonious living. It was taken for granted that good community life existed in these groups as long as individuals had the discipline and the charity to cooperate with each other. By the time of the Council, the trend toward understanding the witness of community life from a theological base was already in place as shown by such articles as Robert Kruse, "Community Life: Witness to Christ" (September, 1965) and Sister Helen Marie, "Toward a Theology of Community," (September, 1965). These few articles foreshadowed the efforts of the coming years regarding the development of vital community living in religious communities.

An interesting phenomenon in the pre-Vatican II *Review* is the large number of articles on the psychological aspects of religious life. Major trends in these articles are the use of psychological testing as a means of screening candidates to religion (S.M. Digna: May 1950, May 1951; William Bier: November 1953, January 1954; R. Vaughan: March 1957);

psychological problems and mental illness among religious (Vaughan: January 1959, March 1960; John Wain: March 1961; P. Rond: January 1962); and psychological needs and personal growth of religious (Dubay: November 1962, January 1963; G.D. Maloney: July 1963). Only three sociological studies were published in the fifties, all of these relating exclusively to longevity of men and women in selected religious orders (Schnepp and Kurz, November 1953; Sister Josephine, January 1955; F. Madigan, July 1959).

A final significant group of authors were those who articulated a theology of religious life. This was a new direction in religious writings and did not show up in the periodical literature, at least not that for general readership, until the early 1960s. These articles attempted to explicate for their readers an understanding of religious life as revealed in Scripture, in Tradition and in the teachings of the Church. Such an approach provided a richer understanding of the mystery of this life than had been afforded by earlier considerations of the practice of the Rule and the regulations of Canon Law. The best representatives of this group of writers are Yves Congar, "The Theology of Religious Women" (January 1960); Henry Holstein, "The Mystery of Religious Life" (September 1961); J. Tillard, "Religious Life in the Mystery of the Church" (November 1963); "Religious Life: Sign of the Eschatological Church" (March 1964); "Religious Life: Sacrament of God's Presence (January 1964); Eugene Bianchi, "Religious Life and the Paschal Mystery" (March 1964) and Gustave Martelet, "The Church's Holiness and Religious Life" (November 1965).

Besides the *Review for Religious* the historian of renewal in religious orders should examine the periodical *Sponsa Regis*, renamed *Sisters Today* in 1965, a journal devoted primarily to the devotional/spiritual growth of religious women. There are several noteworthy articles pertinent to renewal from the pre-Council era. Sister Mary Emil, IHM of the Sister Formation movement wrote a series of three articles on the apostolate of teaching in the light of the renewal movement in the Church (April, May, June, 1961). Particularly informative is Sister Mary Richardine's account of the beginnings of Sister Formation up to 1960, which sheds light on the ideas and persons involved in this early renewal effort (April, 1962). Karl Rahner published a series of four articles on poverty (July—August 1962) which highlighted some of the questions related to religious poverty in the modern world.

A survey of the pre-Vatican religious literature shows that changes in religious orders in the 1950's were initiated by higher authority. The changes proposed by Rome dealt with adaptation of such external practices as flexibility in the order of the convent day, elimination of outmoded ascetical practices, provision for better professional training, and modification of religious garb. First and foremost, they proposed renewal of religious spirit — better religious formation and a deepened understanding of the vowed commitment by religious. Superiors were enjoined by the Pope and the Sacred Congregation of Religious to effect these changes in a gradual and orderly manner.

As the sixties opened and preparation for the Council began, religious literature shows the change. Noticeable was an increase in writings dealing with renewal of spirit, personal growth, theological understanding of the vows, and examination of the role of religious in the Church. Vatican II affected religious writings even before it opened and certainly while it was in process. It would, as a matter of fact, affect the lives of religious women and the writings on religious life for a long time to come.

Chapter Two

VATICAN COUNCIL AND AFTER

It is certainly an understatement to say that the sixties and early seventies in the United States were times of unrest. True as that was in society at large, it was also true in the Church and in religious orders. The country was rocked by the turmoil of a long-coming civil rights movement. As the sixties opened, four black students in Greensboro, N.C. protested the local custom of not serving lunch to a seated black person and set off a national movement of protest. James Meredith's struggle to attend "Ole Miss" in 1962 highlighted the white bastion that education in America really was. Between it all, a youthful President Kennedy launched his "New Frontier" with much hope and promise, followed quickly by his tragic assassination. Johnson's War on Poverty was soon overshadowed by the War in Vietnam, both of them inconclusive at best. The civil rights movement for blacks and for women escalated along with the war in Southeast Asia. The evening news showed marchers in Selma, cries of Black Power, riots in Watts and Newark, countless Vietnam demonstrations and the daily "body count." At the close of the decade protest was at its peak. Early May, 1970, brought Cambodia and Kent State. Even as Americans had become more and more dependent on the structures of authority, they were now becoming more and more critical of that authority, challenging it on all levels — in government, in corporations, in university, and in church. A closer analysis of the turmoil, disorganization, and revolt showed that society was in process of recasting social values and reorganizing social structures to effect a wider distribution of authority, especially in the policy-making process. The developing value system would recognize the individual's need and desire for a voice in issues which would affect his/her life. This challenge to authority began a process of decentralization that emphasized individual freedom, individual expression, and individual responsibility. It was not a trend that would pass when American youth doffed their cast-off army shirts and jeans for more conventional clothing. It was to evolve and become part of the social fabric of the late twentieth century, one that would affect every institution in the land, including religious orders. William Meissner analyzed this cultural phenomenon in *Assault on Authority* (Orbis, 1971). He followed his discussion of authority and its mechanisms and distortions in the sixties with a consideration of the ramifications this had on authority and obedience in religious communities.

The social climate in the Church paralleled the nation's unrest. John XXIII had been Pope for only ninety days when he announced on January 25, 1959, that he would convoke the Church's Twenty-first Ecumenical Council. After four years of careful preparation, on October 11, 1962, the Council opened. Four sessions and sixteen documents later, the Fathers of the Council had taken a serious look at the Church and her role in the world. As the Council closed on December 8, 1965, its work was really only beginning. The documents promulgated by the Council Fathers were noteworthy for their concern for the poor and for their emphasis on the unity of the whole human family. They repeatedly emphasized the obligation of the Christian to build a just and peaceful world order. Noteworthy, too, were the concepts of the people of God as stated in the document on the Church (*Lumen Gentium*), the universal call to holiness, and collegiality, a completely new interpretation of the exercise of authority in the Church.

The two Council documents on the Church, *Lumen Gentium* and *Gaudium et Spes*, were basic to an understanding of renewed religious life after the Council. These documents defined the Church and her role in today's world, and discussed religious life within the context of the total church. *Lumen Gentium* (November 21, 1964) emphasized the concept of the Church as the new People of God (ch. 2), whose heritage is the dignity and freedom of the sons (and daughters) of God and whose goal is the building of the Kingdom of God on earth. The Council Fathers called the whole church to holiness (ch. 5) and made it clear "that all the faithful. . . are called to the fullness of the Christian life and to the perfection of charity" —bishops, priests, deacons, married couples, religious, laborers, even those who are oppressed. Religious, as members of the People of God, work with laity and clergy for the building of the Kingdom (ch. 6). *Gaudium et Spes* reiterated the concept of the People of God, the solidarity of the whole human family and the dignity of the human person (ch. 2), and discussed at length the relationship and duties of the Church, as People of God, to the secular world.

In his address "To All Religious" (May 23, 1964) Pope Paul VI recognized the "universal vocation of all the Faithful to holiness of life," but emphasized the importance of the religious state, "a state of life which keeps in view the constant growth of charity." He reminded religious of the need to study the spirit of their founders, to renew the government structures of their institutes, to change the rules of their institute to meet modern conditions, and to renew their spiritual life.

The most famous document (from the Council years) for renewal of religious life is *Perfectae Caritatis*, the Decree on the Adaptation and Renewal of Religious Life (October 28, 1965). The Council Fathers established two norms for this renewal — the Gospels and the spirit of the founder (art. 2) — and made a distinction between adaptation (the change in external structures and practices) and renewal (the renovation of the interior spirit). They emphasized the importance of having the cooperation of all members for successful renewal and required that superiors "consult the members and give them a hearing." The heart of the document is found in the articles on the vows (12-14) and on community life (15).

A useful commentary on these conciliar documents related to religious life was Francis Cortese's dissertation *Religious Life According to Vatican Council II* (Rome, May, 1968). Cortese discussed the history of *Lumen Gentium* and *Perfectae Caritatis*, as they evolved during the Council. Noting the debates at each phase of the document's evolution, he noted that *Lumen Gentium* is a constitution and that *Perfectae Caritatis*, because of its disciplinary and practical nature, is a decree. As such, *Perfectae Caritatis* did not propose a theology of religious life; *Lumen Gentium* had presented that. The purpose of *Perfectae Caritatis* was rather to set forth general principle for the renewal of religious life (p. 40).

Friedrich Wulf provided a lengthier commentary on *Perfectae Caritatis*, available in *A Commentary on the Documents of Vatican II* (Vol. II), edited by Herbert Vorgrimler (pp. 301-370). His work discussed at greater depth the evolution of the document during the Council, citing the nature of the diverse interpretations brought to the floor for discussion and the votes cast on the various drafts. Wulf then commented at some length on the decree, article by article.

The Religious Life Defined by Ralph Wiltgen (Techny, 1970) was a translation of the official commentary on the chapter about religious in *Lumen Gentium*. The book outlined the process of formulating this chapter, including comments of the bishops and the doctrinal commission on each draft, along with results of votes taken. Wiltgen's comments, clearly indicated as such in the text, facilitate the reader's understanding of the issues involved.

These are the most important documents from the Council for research on religious life. Equally important were two documents issued after the Council. In August 1966 Paul VI issued *Ecclesiae Sanctae*, the enabling legislation for four

Council decrees, among them *Perfectae Caritatis*. The norms proposed for the implementation of these documents were promulgated on an experimental basis. The document emphasized that the most important role in renewal was that of the orders themselves and that this renewal should be accomplished not merely by making laws, but by encouraging the participation of both superiors and members. Each order was to hold a special meeting of its highest body, the general chapter, and should prepare for it by full and free consultation with all members. This special body had the right to suspend and/or alter certain practices of the order's Rule. From this should evolve a complete revision of the Constitution or Rule of the order, taking care that members be heard from on a continuing basis.

Three years later, in February 1969, the Sacred Congregation of Religious issued *Renovationis Causam*, a document concerning the training of those entering religious orders. The document, like *Ecclesiae Sanctae*, allowed experimentation and set out in broad guidelines the principles for this training, encouraging greater flexibility and broader experience during this time of probation.

Religious orders struggled with renewal and adaptation in life style, dress, and community life. Expansion of apostolic works and the revision of Constitutions became well known features for religious women. Documents from the Holy See continued to give direction to renewal. In *Evangelica Testificatio* on the Renewal of Religious Life, issued in 1971, Paul VI reminded religious of the essential commitment of the vows and especially the obligation of religious to respond to the cry of the poor for justice. He called them to a deepened spiritual renewal and to an evangelical witness in today's world. He commended the orders that had begun in earnest the process of renewal, in some cases, he said, "too hardily." In this document the Pope focused primarily on interior revitalization of religious spirit and a renewed dedication to vowed life in community.

The later addresses of Paul VI reflected the concern that many had for developments in religious life. In October, 1972, and November, 1973, the Pope again spoke to Major

Superiors of Men and Women of the need for interior renewal beyond the changes in structures. He called them to be faithful to their "religious spirit," in the face of many changes in style and form of religious living.

At the opening of the sixties membership in religious orders continued to increase each year, but by the end of the Council, and the years following, it was apparent that there were fewer young women entering the orders. By 1966 membership reached a high of 181,421. By 1970 it had dropped to 160,931 and in 1975 the *Official Catholic Directory* registered 135,225 religious women in the United States. The decrease was not only due to fewer new entrants; it was brought on in large part by a continuous exodus from convents the nation over.

The documents of the Council Fathers, along with the social climate of the sixties, had brought the message of renewal to the rank and file of sisters in religious orders. Society of the sixties questioned social institutions, and with the renewed call from the Council for change, the convent too, as institution, was subject to scrutiny. The role, even the relevance and authenticity, of religious life was questioned. Religious women sought a new meaning for their vows of obedience, poverty and celibacy in a changing and modern world. Organization structures such as habit, horarium, and community life were modified or even radically altered. To be considered as a person with social, psychological, and spiritual needs was a new experience to women schooled to taking a second place to the cause of the religious order. The delicate balance of community and apostolate was tipped almost continually in favor of apostolate, pointing to a need for a better understanding of an apostolic spirituality, or an integration of the active and contemplative life of the religious woman.

The Conference of Major Superiors, responsible for the leadership of American religious women, sought to clarify and analyze the position of the membership on these numerous issues. In August 1965 CMSW approved a study to determine the readiness of sisters for planned programs in renewal and to decide what direction this planning should

take. (Neal, *Review of Religious Research*, V. 11, p. 5).
Sociologist Sr. Maria Augusta Neal, S.N.D., headed the
research team which created the instrument and analyzed
the data. In 1967 a twenty-three page survey (649 questions)
was sent to 157,000 religious women in the United States.
Eighty-eight percent (88%), almost 140,000 responded. The
survey tested the relationship between beliefs, attitudes and
readiness for change and included a pre- and post-Vatican
belief scale, a measure of anomie, authoritarianism, political pessimism, attitudes towards values, interest and
change, and a direct measure of prejudice. (See Neal, RRR.
V. 11, p. 7.) The study supported the hypothesis that beliefs
are causal factors in readiness to accept or resist change. A
lengthy section on Census Data and Community (Section
V) made possible a profile of each congregation on apostolic
works, age levels, reading habits, experience with the poor,
preferences of life styles, involvement in the secular world,
to name only a few. Within two months each community
received its frequency printout by percentage and number,
along with national scores for comparison. Neal published
her report on the project in two parts in *Review of Religious
Research* (Part I: Vol. 11, 1970; II: Vol. 12, 1971) "The
Relation Between Religious Belief and Structural Change."
She discussed her methodology at length in Part I; the
second part gave the results of her testing. This survey is a
rich resource for understanding religious women of active
orders in the United States in the mid-sixties.

The publications of the years after the Council reflected
the social and religious climate. The Theology Department
of the University of Notre Dame continued in-service programs for Sisters in their Institute for Local Superiors held
annually from 1962 to 1966. The published *Proceedings*
(Ed. Robert Pelton, 1962-1963; Albert Schlitzer, ed. 1964-
1966) revealed the same multifaceted interest and expertise
as their earlier institutes of spirituality. The University of
Portland sponsored a similar program from 1960 to 1963,
which resulted in the publication of selected papers in four
volumes: Joseph Haley, *The Sisters in America Today, The
Religious and the Vatican Council, New Directions for*

Religious Life and *Mental Health and Religious* (University of Notre Dame Press, 1965).

Symposia and institutes on religious life abounded in the sixties. Some resulted in publications; others simply drew large and interested crowds seeking answers. The common thread of the symposia was an effort not to give answers but to further investigation into questions on religious life. Gerald Huyghe's publication *Religious Orders in the Modern World* (1965) dealt with the definition of religious life, its place in the Church, and the principles and practice of renewal in orders. The collection, written by several bishops and theologians in attendance at the Council, was inspired by the debates in the Council concerning the schema on the Church and religious life. Karl Rahner's contribution, "The Theology of Religious Life," pointed out the need to face the differences of interpretation and to continue to seek answers to the meaning and place of religious life in the Church. He investigated religious life through the prism of the universal call to holiness expected of all the people of God.

The articles in *Problems That Unite Us* (1966) were papers presented at an institute of the B.V.M. Sisters in Mundelein, Illinois. Originally the publication was intended only for their sisters. Requests from many other congregations prompted a wider distribution of the book.

A last example of the institute publications is *Vows But No Walls* (1967), edited by Eugene Grollmes. This institute at St. Louis University concentrated on interpretations and meaning of the vows and community life. Again the contributors were well-known men and women, most of them in religious orders, speaking from a diversity of disciplines.

Useful tools for the researcher are the publictions derived directly from the Roman documents. Elio Gambari, long involved in renewal, published *Renewal in Religious Life* (St. Paul's, 1967) which dealt with the content and purpose of *Perfectae Caritatis* and *Ecclesiae Sanctae* in their relation to religious formation. Of his two works on formation written in the sixties, only his second one, *The Updating of Religious Formation* (St. Paul's, 1969), directly responds to *Renovationis Causam*. His earlier work, *Religious Apos-*

tolic Formation for Sisters (Fordham, 1964) was mostly a systematic statement of the basic principles involved in formation as he had presented them to various Sister Formation audiences of an earlier time. In 1967, The Daughters of St. Paul compiled a volume, *Religious Life in the Light of Vatican II*, containing the papal documents with selected commentaries, followed in 1974 with a similar volume *Documents on Renewal*. Their 1970 volume *Fidelity and Relevance* presented the thoughts of Paul VI on renewal — its theological essence, its interior quality and its dynamics. The 325 excerpts are taken from the Pontiff's pronouncements in the post-Conciliar period. Out of concern for too great emphasis on adaptation of external practice rather than interior renewal, Rose Eileen Masterson edited *Religious Life: A Mystery in the Church* (Alba House, 1975) in which she placed renewal in the context of the Church's magisterium.

Studies in the psychology of the religious person blossomed after the Council, continuing an earlier trend in religious writing and reflecting as well the interest in the person during the sixties. Well received were publications of Adrian van Kaam of Duquesne University and those of John Evoy and Van Christoph. Van Kaam's books, among them *Religion and Personality* (Prentice-Hall, 1964), *Personality Fulfillment in the Spiritual Life* (Dimension, 1966) and *The Vowed Life* (Dimension, 1968), approached the topic through the psychology of religion and personality theory. John J. Evoy and Van F. Christoph dealt mainly with personality development and maturity in religious life. Their books, *Personality Development in Religious Life* (Sheed and Ward, 1963), *Maturity in Religious Life* (1965) and *The Real Woman in Religious Life* (1967) were told in dialogue form and evolved from conferences given at the Institute of Applied Psychology.

Marian Robinson's *Creative Personality in Religious Life* (Sheed and Ward, 1963) and William Meissner's *Group Dynamics in Religious Life* (Notre Dame Press, 1965) reflected some of the same ideas as Evoy and van Kaam. Robinson treated the topic from the perspective of the individual's own psychology. Meissner dealt with the solidarity of community and group participation. In 1971 Charles Curran (*Psychological Dynamics in Religious Living*) pointed to a need to "re-personalize" religious institutional structures to serve individuals rather than some abstraction.

The discussion of psychological assessment of prospective candidates for religious life continued in John Ford, *Religious Superior, Subject and Psychiatrists* (1963), dealing with questions of personal privacy relative to such tests. A workshop for psychologists engaged in such testing sponsored in 1966 by the Center for Applied Research in the Apostolate (CARA), resulted in the publication of *Assessment of Candidates for Religious Life* (1968). Besides providing sample assessment reports, the book discussed the purposes of these tests, the responsibilities of those involved, and gave direction on the planning of assessment programs. Robert McAllister in *Conflict in Community* (1969) discussed the same topic, not so much to understand the process and results of testing, but to give the individual a better understanding of the role of early family life in her personality development, her self-acceptance, her relationships with others, and her ability to cope with stress in community life. To McAllister psychological testing made sense only if religious communities used it for the sake of the community alone. Psychological screening of candidates entering orders became a reality for some communities in the late sixties. Books such as these were timely aids to those orders contemplating or using this practice.

Beyond the categories described in the books so far noted, it is hard to delineate the emphasis in the plethora of books written on religious life in the sixties. Besides the common theme of the nun in the modern world, one finds a strong emphasis on structural renewal and an attempt simply to understand what is going on. Many present an overview of religious life — vocation, the vows, community life, the apostolate — explicitly noting that they are not presenting a full theology of religious life. In this sense there is a transitional character to these books.

Cardinal Suenens' *The Nun in the World* led this group of

publications (1963). Written during the Council, the book
pointed to all aspects of renewal — the need for more
involvement of religious in the Church's apostolate, for
balance between prayer and the apostolate, for provision
for adequate spiritual and professional training for religious, and for revision of constitutions. Almost as popular
as Suenens were Sister Charles Borromeo Muckenhirn's
books, *The Changing Sister* (Notre Dame, 1965) and *The
New Nuns* (New American Library, 1967). As editor of
these works Muckenhirn brought together representative
writers, almost all of them religious women, to discuss a
wide variety of questions on religious life. The contributors,
of recognized competence in their fields of the humanities
and social sciences, addressed the major questions of religious life in the sixties. Their articles responded to the
Vatican II documents on the Church and religious life,
especially the concept of the People of God and the universal call to holiness. Topics presented in these two books
dealt with change in the sisters' life style and community
structures, the need for personal development of the sisters,
apostolic work especially in the inner city and in peace
efforts, and the need for a better understanding of religious
life through study of Scripture and liturgy. The authors
discussed the questions of change from the perspective of
many disciplines — psychology, sociology, theology, history — and clarified the salient issues inherent in the renewal process. All the articles are thought-provoking and of
interest, even today. Although it is difficult to point out any
one article without mentioning many more, I note Sr. Marie
Augusta Neal's article, "Religious Communities in a Changing World" (*New Nuns*, p. 142), which addressed the condit-
ons of modern society and the need for change in religious
orders. Her sociological discussion of six trends in modern-
day living gave insight into the relationshps of the orders to
contemporary society. Muckenhirn's comments in a con-
cluding chapter "The On-Going Dialogue" sum up the experience of renewal for religious at that time, pointing out that
religious life is still what it always was — freely chosen
dedication to God. The mode of this dedication is evolving,

she said, and "will be clarified slowly through failure as well as success." (p. 206)

These two books are still among the most pertinent today to understand renewal in religious orders from its many perspectives. Muckenhirn presented her own further reflections on renewal more extensively in her last book, *Implications for Renewal* (Notre Dame, 1967), in which she placed renewal in the context of Christian revolution and reflected on the meaning of renewal in the vowed life, in the apostolate, in Church and in society. Her reflections elucidated the message of Vatican II on renewal for the Church, for the People of God and especially for religious women. She was keenly in touch with the controversies within and outside the Church regarding renewal. She summed up much of her thought in the last chapter: "Most of all [the religious woman of the future] will be a woman of Vatican II, trying to live the gospels in all their power and relevance within the actual cultural and human needs of the persons who come within reach of her love and service." (p. 292)

Several of the more controversial writers of the time were Judith Tate, *Sisters for the World* (Herder and Herder, 1965) and *Religious Women* (1970), Gabriel Moran, *Experience in Community* (1968) and *The New Community* (1970), and Patrick Berkery, *Restructuring Religious Life* (1968). The perspectives of time and experience have moderated attitudes towards such critiques of religious life and the Church, especially since development in the years since their publication brought greater credibility to some of their ideas.

There were still the superficial works, or otherwise outmoded remnants of an earlier age. Hilary Smith, *Realism in Renewal* (1969), provided a "guide to survival for the ordinary sister who is happy in her community but has a few questions." Claude Kean, *As One of Them* (1965), published his letters to his niece under subtitle, *Letters to Sister Superior.* Anselm Romb's *Signs of Contradiction* (1967), had all the earmarks of the old "virtues" books of the fifties, dealing with aspects of religious life in a "chatty" style. Though the book appealed for change, for charity in com-

munities, for adaptation of convent rules, it lacked a solid
base in Scripture, Council documents, and Church tradition. Desmond McGoldrick in *Independence Through Submission* (1964) discussed obedience and consecration of the
religious person. His comment that all women, but especially religious, "contact reality only at the emotional level
... interpret truth on the level of feelings ... which become
the premise for drawing conclusions," left something to be
desired even in 1964.

The decline in vocations was a continued concern in
religious circles. Interest in the meaning of vocation for the
individual and for the Church showed in most publications.
The earliest and best treatment for its time was Charles
Schleck *The Theology of Vocation* (1963), which evolved
from a course Schleck taught for the religious formation
students at Notre Dame. Schleck's book did not discuss the
decline in vocations; rather, based on the Fathers of the
Church, classical spiritual writers such as John of the Cross
and Teresa of Carmel, the Scriptures and Canon Law, it
delved into the meaning of vocation in much the same way
as Rahner presented his theology of religious life. In *Personalism and Vocation* (Alba House, 1966) Germain Lesage
also addressed the meaning and the development of vocation and contemporary trends in terms of vocation. In a
final chapter on religious observance he discussed the
aspects of religious practice that were in need of adaptation.
Ralph Dyer (*The New Religious, an Authentic Image*,
1967), in an effort to evoke a renewed response of generosity
from religious for their vocation, related the traditional
values of the religious life to the insights of contemporary
theology. Possibly the most useful part of Dyer's book is an
extensive bibliography on renewal. Joseph Sikora reap-
praised the meaning of call and examined contemporary
objections to the notion of religious vocation (*Calling*,
1968).

Significant among works on vocation and formation was
Elio Gambari's *The Religious Adult in Christ* (1971). This
new work on the juniorate revealed Gambari's adaptation

to a changing religious life. Rather than emphasizing a time and place for the juniorate, he now focused on the objective of forming a mature Christian person capable of making a perpetual commitment and of accepting the responsibilities of today's apostolic service.

These books on vocation made an attempt to consider their topic in the light of the Council and other papal documents. Some of them have an element of trying to rejuvenate the fervor of vocation without having arrived at a fully renewed understanding of the Lord's call to religious life.

These years after the Council were years of tensions and uneasiness for many religious, tensions wrought by uncertainty, by change and by inability to articulate in a satisfying way the role of religious in Church and world. These tensions were apparent in most of the publications. Noteworthy were Gerard Huyghe's *Tensions and Change* (1966), Sr. Jeanne d'Arc's *Witness and Consecration* (1966), Paul Hinnebusch's *The Signs of the Times and the Religious Life* (1967) and Robert Gleason's *The Restless Religious* (1968). These authors generally dealt with the question of tension directly and in a positive light.

Publications of the early seventies revealed the continued search of religious orders for meaning in their lives (e.g. Jerome Murphy-O'Connor, *What is Religious Life?*). Some authors continued to question the future of religious life; others discussed the crisis in which they found themselves and continued to challenge religious to respond to the call of the Church. Thomas O'Meara (*Holiness and Radicalism in Religious Life*, 1970) and Thomas Clarke (*New Pentecost or New Passion*, 1973) called for a radical stance in living religious life. Radicalism, O'Meara noted, begins with the root demands of being a Christian and living in a Christian apostolic community. Anything not of the Gospel or of the Spirit was to be questioned and replaced. Clarke called religious to a countercultural stance. The first call we religious had, he said, was to "get with it." Now we are called to "get against it." He believed that the Church has an obligation to be critical of American cultural values, and that religious have a crucial role in shaping and expressing this stance.

Books by Donald Gelpi (*Discerning the Spirit*, 1970), Kevin O'Rourke (*Reflections on Renewal*, 1971), and Thomas Dubay (*Can Religious Life Survive?*, 1973) reflected the concerns related to the future of religious life.

Several collections addressed the "crisis" in religious renewal and the need for theological understanding of the religious state. *The Challenge to Religious Life Today* (Colm O'Grady, ed., 1970) considered such disparate topics as the relevance of the teaching sister, the problems of formation, and the biblical foundations of religious life. *Religious Life in the 70's*, edited by Kevin O'Rourke, gave greater emphasis to the social apostolate of religious persons. Peter Huizing and William Bassett edited *The Future of Religious Life* (1975), which took an historical, social, and international perspective. The biblical perspective was dealt with by David Stanley in *Faith and Religious Life* (1971) and by Stephen Doyle in *Covenant Renewal in Religious Life* (1975).

There was little mention of the social climate in the country at large in this literature of renewal. One might believe that the social protests for civil rights did not exist if one had to learn about them from publications about religious life at this time. Though many works included discussions on the apostolate, e.g. Muckenhirn's *The Changing Sister* and *The New Nuns*, only a few works published in this period dealt solely with this topic. Gertrude Donnelly in *The Sister Apostle* (Notre Dame, 1964) presented the role of the religious vis-a-vis the rising apostolate of the laity, with the role that formation played in terms of the apostolate, the necessity to train leaders and to give the young person an apostolic outlook from the beginning. Jacques Leclerc in *The Apostolic Spirituality of the Nursing Sister* (Alba House, 1966) noted the need for the religious nurse to be professionally prepared, but to "be the nun first." *New Works for New Nuns* (1968) edited by Sister M. Peter Traxler was the only book at this time that related to the contemporary social scene and dealt directly with the apostolate to the poor and to those marginalized by society. The chapters were written by nuns involved in works such as Head Start, store front apostolates in poverty sections of cities, and drug rehabilitation programs.

Apparent in the post-Vatican publications is a search by religious writers for a theology of religious life, an attempt to relate the commitment of religious life to Christian living as based on the Gospels, Tradition, and the teachings of the Church. Although the Council provided excellent documents on the church in *Gaudium et Spes* and *Lumen Gentium*, it failed to produce a document of like quality for the religious state. Some writers, for example Francis Maloney (*Disciples and Prophets*, 1981), noted that prior to the Council there was a flourishing theology of the Church on which the council documents built. It is only since the Council that the Church has recognized the need to develop a similar theology for the religious state.

Particularly conscious of the need for a theology of religious life was Elio Gambari who published an academic study in two volumes. In *The Global Mystery of Religious Life* (1970) he dealt with religious life in the total context of the world and the Church. His second volume, *The Unfolding of the Mystery of Religious Life* (1973), developed the covenant character of the religious state, the vows, the community and apostolic life of the religious. Earlier works explicating a theology were J. Tillard, *The Mystery of Religious Life* (1967) and Paul Hinnebusch, *Religious Life: A Living Liturgy* (1965). Thomas Dubay (*Ecclesial Women*, 1970) took a slightly different approach, developing his theology from the focus of "women for the church." He presented what he termed "more than an academic book" showing the theological roots, the functions and implications of being ecclesial women. Robert Faricy in *Spirituality for Religious Life* (1976) emphasized one's relationship with the person of Jesus and the need to integrate faith into active lives.

Periodical Literature

It comes as no surprise that articles in the general category of renewal were among the most frequently published
in the *Review for Religious* in the ten years following the
Council. Many of the articles dealt with the revision or
rewriting of constitutions as mandated by the Sacred Congregation. These articles ranged from "How to Write Good
Constitutions' (L. Orsy, May 1973), which gave the principles and the guidelines necessary for the preparation of a
new rule of life, to published drafts of constitutions in
process, e.g. "Life Charter for the Sisters of the Precious
Blood," (Myerscough and Kurilla, July 1966). The
researcher can get a clear idea of the necessity for the
revision of constitutions by a cursory glance at a few of the
rules used by religious orders prior to Vatican Council II.
Many of the apostolic orders had revised their rules to
conform to the 1918 code of Canon Law. In an effort to be in
line with Church practice most orders had incorporated
large portions of the new canons for Religious into their
rules. The remainder of the rule tended to be the "do's" and
"don't's" of living in a religious order. Vatican Council II's
emphasis on the need for religious orders to get in touch
with their unique charism and to incorporate this into a
revised rule led to more pastoral constitutions, ones which
specifically reflected the special character of the order and
exhorted members to live the ideal of religious life. Statutes
and by-laws to these constitutions included more specific
regulations. The history of the constitutions or rules of an
order can give valuable insight into the character of an order
and of religious life. Such aspects as interpretations of the
essentials of religious life, the methods of regulatory practice, the use of language and the changes in organizational
structures frequently reflect the social history of an age and
reveal attitudes of the Church and the order that have social
significance. Preparing for and planning change, reorganizing government structures, studying the charism of the
founders, experimentation with community forms and with
adaptation of the habit were other subjects frequently

treated in the periodical literature. Of special value to the researcher is "Bibliography for Renewal" (January 1967) by Damien Isabell and Brother Joachim, which provides references to articles on renewal under several categories.

The articles on community life, another very much discussed topic, reflected much of the reality in religious life at the time when sisters sought a deeper meaning in their life in common. Many sisters came to realize that the quality of their time together in community was more important than the traditional practice of all members following a set daily schedule. The articles looked at many facets of communal life — the witness quality, the human dimensions, polarization in community, sharing of faith. Several articles discussed the notion of unity in diversity (e.g. Mayeski, May 1974) or pluralism (Regan, 1973; Keane, 1973; Nuij, 1973), foreshadowing the changes that would ultimately evolve in the lived reality of community life. The large number of articles on the subject of common life reflected the concern, even the anxiety, about experimentation in communal structures. Religious women in these years investigated the outside world with enthusiasm and followed the mandate of Rome to experiment with new forms. Frequently enough individual sisters did not wait for those in authority to make the first move or, faced with reluctance on the part of the superior, made their own decisions. This was a source of anxiety to some and of confusion to many others. What constitutes good community life was the question of concern. Some sisters found the demands of an unadjustable schedule of prayer and meal times inhibiting to the work of a particular apostolate. Flexibility in the order of the day for the individual who needed to adjust these times in order to serve the People of God better was one of the desires of many sisters in the active apostolate. Other sisters were less willing to adapt to a more flexible horarium, and often had questions concerning the kind of apostolates some sisters had entered, especially those which made such demands on the sisters. The articles in the *Review* reflect these concerns. Spiritual/theological reflections on community life (Schleck, July 1966; Grosh, January 1974; Doohan, 1974), investigation of other forms of common life (e.g. Fleck, September, 1971; Nuij, 1973), and the problems of polarization and conflict (O'Meara, March 1971; M. Eleanor, January 1969) were several of the emphases in these studies on community life.

If there was fear by some that the spiritual life was neglected in the renewal process, the large number of articles on growth in this very important area of religious life in no way indicated neglect. Articles dealing with prayer, of notable increase beginning in the early 1970's, showed an interest in deepening the prayer life of the individual religious, emphasizing not so much an intellectual understanding but a reflection on meaning, experience and disposition for prayer. Related to this was the interest in improving the annual retreat of sisters. Through these years there was a significant change made in the forms of retreats from the preached retreat given to a large number of sisters to the directed retreat, an individual relationship of retreatant to director. The retreatant's daily conference with the director concerning her response to the day's prayer made possible greater personal responsiblity and a deepening of the sister's spiritual life. The articles in the *Review* as early as 1966 speak to this development; like the articles on prayer, retreat articles show a significant increase in the early 1970's.

The vows and the theology of religious life continued as a topic of the *Review*'s articles. Chastity received the greatest attention if one judges by quantity of articles. Indeed, celibacy needed a much better understanding among religious. Many of those who left religious orders during this time gave the desire to marry as their reason for leaving religious life. Authors of the periodical literature treated the topic in its theological/scriptural aspects (e.g. Sarno, 1970; Dubay, 1968), its psychological aspects (Flaherty, "Psychological Needs of Celibates," 1970), the dimensions of human love (e.g. Sikora, "Chastity and Love," 1968; Ranger, "Love Has its Properties," 1968; "Meaning and Function of Sex for Celibates," 1975).

The smaller number of articles on religious obedience should not mislead the researcher into interpreting this as a declining interest in this vow. Rather, as Thomas Dubay and Thomas Clancy pointed out in separate articles (July, 1974), the confusion in the meaning and role of authority and the lack of willingness on the part of religious to accept the authority of the superior as understood in the past prompted some authors to shy away from such topics. Both the above-mentioned authors place this crisis of obedience into the context of the authority crisis in society at large. In spite of a growing tendency toward democracy in religious orders, Clancy cited first Rahner's statement that religious life can never be totally democratized and secondly *Evangelica Testificatio*, which stated that superiors must have personal authority. These years in the history of religious life, as the articles attest, were difficult for those in authority inside and outside religious orders. The confusion and, in some cases, strong feelings concerning authority were possible reasons for fewer articles on obedience, as Dubay particularly noted.

Emphasis in the articles dealing with the psychological aspects of religious life paralleled, to a large extent, the emphasis given in the book publications cited earlier. There are fewer publications after 1970 on psychological testing programs for those entering religious orders. This may mean that most arguments, for and against had been presented, or that orders had by now made up their minds one way or another on this topic. It is probably safe to say that by the present (1983) most religious orders use some kind of testing program to assess abilities of those seeking entrance to their communities. The greatest emphasis of the psychological articles was on the general development of the person and, in particular, on the psychological aspects of the religious/ spiritual life, e.g. community living, celibacy, formation.

Noteworthy in new topics treated in the *Review* in the ten years after the Council were articles on retirement, on departures from religious life and on women in the ministry of the Church, particularly the ordination of women to the priesthood. Each of these topics would find greater visibility in future publications.

Chapter Three

RECENT TRENDS

By the mid-seventies the nation had withdrawn from the controversial war in Southeast Asia and had weathered the corruption of the Watergate scandal. Americans had seemingly settled into what some described as the new conservatism of the seventies, akin to that of the 1950's. An examination of the record indicates that changes, perhaps more significant than many realized, were going on . Noticeable was an increased awareness of the rights of the person shown in such events as the Privacy Act and the Freedom of Information Act in mid-decade. The right of the handicapped to equal education (1975) and greater sanctions against those who refused to desegregate schools were other evidences. Women continued to seek their place in society amid a host of controversial issues related to family , marriage, and the home. The abortion controversy opened wide with the Supreme Court case of 1973. The divorce rate and the number of illegitimate births rose at a faster pace than in the 1960's. The 1980 census indicated a significant rise of 79% in one-parent households, one of every five families with children cared for by one parent (U.S. Statistical Abstracts). Extension of the Voting Rights Act in 1975 to include Hispanics, American Indians, and Asian-Americans reflected the fact that immigration into the United States in the seventies was the greatest since the pre-exclusion decade 1911-1920.

If John Naisbitt in *Megatrends* (Warner Books, 1982) is right, the United States was shifting from an industrial to a service/information-oriented nation, balancing "high-tech" with "high-touch" and becoming more interdependent with other nations, rather than being the dominant independent power it once was. Business was diversifying and decentralization of institutions accelerating, bringing about more dependence of the individual on him/herself, and more participation of the individual in the political process, especially on the local and state levels. Greater communication through networking evolved from self-help and participatory democracy movements, strengthening each other in the process.

The melting pot myth, already cracked in the sixties with the rise of civil rights and Black Power, shattered as the new influx of immigration, especially from non-Western countries and Latin America, changed the face of America's cities and towns. The recognition of diversity allowed for the celebration of ethnicity and retention of ethnic customs. Even though English remained the dominant language, by 1980 America was moving towards being bi-lingual with Hispanic groups more and more in evidence.

It was not a settled-in era; even less was it a time devoid of tensions. Unemployment and inflation ran at a constantly high level. Many Americans felt that the poor and those marginalized by society had been forgotten by those in power. The threat of nuclear might and the arms build-up loomed larger than ever, threatening not just the peace of the world but its very existence.

By 1980 the Catholics of the United States numbered 22½% of the population, or almost 50 million, actually a decline percentage-wise from a decade earlier. Through the seventies the institutional church had continued its move toward renewal in liturgical reform, in development of sacramental practice, in its legal code, in organizational structures, and particularly in participation of the laity in the ministry of the Church. It was no longer as easy for the

Catholic of this era to define Catholic dogma precisely. Opinion and research polls estimated that Catholic practice too had suffered, if that familiar indicator of weekly Mass attendance continued to be a reliable measure of Catholic vitality. (See James Hennessey, *American Catholics*, Ch. 21.) Issues of right-to-life on all levels — abortion, euthanasia, capital punishment and war — divided the Church within itself and from others.

From another point of view there were those who believed that, in spite of the Church's problems, the quality of parish life in many cases was considerably improved. The laity participated in the life of the parish as members of parish boards, as teachers in the parochial school or in religious education programs, as financial advisors, even in the liturgical life of the parish as lay lectors and special ministers of Communion. For many, the parish worked together as a community of believers, sharing greater responsibility for the needs of the parish and for each other.

The numbers of those who entered the religious profession (men and women) those entering seminaries, and the numbers of men ordained for ministry had declined when compared even to 1970. Lay members of the Church took on some of the functions once performed by religious and priests, a trend noticeable most of all in the schools and hospitals once staffed almost completely by religious women. By 1980 religious sisters numbered 126,000, the decrease now caused more by the decline in numbers entering than by the exodus experienced a decade earlier. A noteworthy development of the late seventies and early eighties was that religious women moved into different apostolic works to meet new needs and often lived in smaller religious communities or even, in some cases, alone. They worked in diocesan centers, as directors of education or newly established diocesan Social Concerns offices, in diocesan marriage tribunals and family services. Even with fewer members religious communities reached out to care for the materially poor and those marginated in other ways by society — e.g. shelter care for women and children and care of the physically and mentally disabled.

Religious women joined with other women to improve the position of women in Church and society. This was noticeably an issue that cut across various group lines, lay and religious, Protestant and Catholic. The issue was larger than the ordination of women to the priesthood, even though such groups as the Women's Ordination Conference and the presence of significant numbers of women students in Catholic seminaries helped keep that issue before the public. Catholic women, among them many religious, continued to pursue higher degrees in theology, giving them at least equal academic qualifications with male theologians in the Church.

By the late seventies and early eighties the work of renewal was not complete in religious orders any more than it was complete in the Church at large. Many orders, though not all, had completed the preparation of new Constitutions. Some had received final approval from the Sacred Congregation of Religious. Most had made the necessary adaptations of the externals of convent life to accommodate different apostolic needs. Unity in diversity (John Naisbitt called it "multiple options") was perhaps one of the outstanding characteristics of the modern religious life — diversity of works combined with a unity of their purpose as religious and with concern for the quality of community life. Evident certainly was the fact that religious women had now taken leadership in determining the direction of religious life in the future.

Documents from Rome regarding renewal of religious life in the late seventies and early eighties added little that was new to the many previous announcements. John Paul II's greatest emphasis in his many addresses to groups of religious centered on two themes: personal consecration and the ecclesial nature of religious life. His writings showed his concern that religious retain the stance of service to the Church and guard against secularization, which could come from losing sight of their ecclesial purpose of apostolic service and personal dedication. Typical of John Paul's thought was his homily (November 14, 1979) to the International Union of Superiors General in which he cautioned against "certain practical choices" which "have not offered the world the true image of Christ." He called religious to fervent and persevering prayer, to witness their faithfulness to the Church through community life and through religious garb. One notices in reading John Paul's messages to religious that he repeats in each document the same ideas in one form or another. He repeats, too, his request that they "evaluate objectively and humbly the years of experimentation so as to recognize their positive elements and their deviations." (IUSG, 1979)

Very helpful to the researcher are two volumes which collate John Paul's addresses on religious life: *Visible Signs of the Gospel* (St. Paul's, 1980) and *Faithfulness to the Gospel* (St. Paul's 1982). It should come as no surprise that the Pontiff in his latest document, his letter to the Bishops of the United States (April 3, 1983), stated again as necessary elements the ecclesial nature of the religious vocation, the witness of public vows and an approved form of community life, the need for fidelity to the founder's charism and to personal and liturgical prayer. This letter took on something of a controversial character in that the Pope appointed a commission of bishops "to help the religious of your country... to live their ecclesial vocation to the full," and asked the bishops to work with the forthcoming document from the Sacred Congregation on the essential elements of religious life.

Efforts have been made to analyze and interpret John Paul's thought, notable among them the John Paul Symposium at Trinity College, Washington, D.C. (1980). One of the resulting publications, *The Pastoral Vision of John Paul II*, edited by Sister Joan Bland (Franciscan Herald Press, 1982) presented the papers given on the impact of the Pope's thought on contemporary realities. Particularly pertinent to this study was Sister Joan Gormley's paper, "On Religious Life" (p. 67), in which, through the prism of Vatican II documents and the Pope's call to fidelity, she discussed his major themes of the personal consecration of religious and his concept of the ecclesial nature of the religious vocation. The personalism pervading the philosophical thought of the

Pope is seen, Gormley noted, in his conviction that love is the ultimate principle of self realization, that religious consecration fosters the human maturation of the person, and that the adventure of the person in religious life is the departure from self and the recovery of self in God.

The ecclesial dimension of the religious vocation means that the consecration of religious persons to God is "in and for the Church;...their mission is a participation in the Church's own." (p. 75) John Paul calls for the expression of this ecclesial dimension through fidelity to the community's charism which is not a separate grace to a community group, but rather a manner of participation and communion with the church. It is, Gormley noted, "nothing less than fidelity to the Church itself for whom the gift was granted in the first place." (p. 76). Of importance to the ecclesial dimension is the participation of religious in the prophetic gift of the Church. According to John Paul, the chief expression of the prophetic gift for religious should be in the witness of holiness of life. The Pope does not deny that religious should be involved in social concerns, but he does insist that these activities be within the evangelical mission of the Church.

Gormley's article is an important one for the researcher. An examination of her analysis of John Paul's thought reveals some of the controversial issues with which religious women in the United States struggle today.

Further discussion of the Pope's ideas about religious life can be found in Barbara Albrecht, "A Pope For Religious" (*Review for Religious*, November 1982), David O'Connor, "Religious and Politics" (RFR, November, 1982), and David Fleming, "Religious in the Service of the Church" (RFR, September, 1982).

Reflecting the greater involvement of religious women in the social issues of the time, in April, 1978, the Sacred Congregation of Religious addressed members of religious orders on the topic of "Religious and Human Concerns." The four concerns set out in the document were the option for the poor and for justice in today's world, the social activities and works of religious as the means to evangelization, the pastoral concern of the Church for the working world, and the need in some way to take a political stance short of direct involvement in politics. In March, 1980, the Sacred Congregation issued a related document, "The Contemplative Dimension of Religious Life," this time underscoring the necessity of a deep spiritual life as basis for the active life of the religious.

The most recent of the documents from the Sacred Congregation, "The Essential Elements in the Church's Teaching on Religious Life"(May 31, 1983), came as a companion piece to John Paul II's April 3 directive to the Bishops of the United States. Its purpose was "to present...a clear statement of the Church's teaching regarding religious life at a moment which is particularly significant and opportune." The Sacred Congregation spoke of the end of the period of experimentation with the completion of the revised code of canon law. The document reiterated the characteristics of religious life: consecration by vows, community life, evangelical mission, prayer, asceticism, public witness, and relation to the Church. A final section included the articles of the new code of canon law pertinent to religious orders.

Religious in the United States reacted in various ways to this document and to the appointment of the Bishops' Commission. At this writing the work of the commission has proceeded, not without tension-filled moments, but with a certain positive thrust. Pertinent to this topic are several noteworthy articles in *Review For Religious* (Vol. 43, No. 2): John Quinn, "The Pastoral Service of Bishops to Religious"; John Sheets, "The Call to the Renewal of Religious Life"; and John Paul II, "A Call to Collegiality in the Service of Religious." Quinn's article provides insight into the mission given the Bishops' Commission, their interpretation of and attitudes towards their mission. Sheets presents the procedures used by the Bishops in commencing the work of the Commission. He provides also his assessment of the attitudes of American religious regarding the Commission, toward the document, and toward the present need for renewal of religious orders.

By the late seventies, publications on religious life as a

whole placed a greater emphasis on the internalization of renewal, a deepening of prayer, a call to more radical living (e.g. David Knight, *Cloud by Day, Fire by Night*; Alejandro Cassianovich, *Religious Life and the Poor*, 1979). There was present in some of these writings a concern for too great a "secularization" of religious life. Most of the publications followed from the principles of the Council, particularly its significant concepts of the People of God and the universal call to holiness. No longer were religious presented as living a "higher life." They, like the laity, were one group within the People of God, all of whom are called to holiness of life. Understandably, then, most of the books on the spiritual life were no longer addressed only to religious as they had been in the pre-Vatican Church. Now they were simply addressed to all Christians interested in the development of a deeper spiritual life. Religious commitment and the vows remained a topic of interest to writers. In a day when many asked questions about "temporary vocations" and the human possibility of promising anything forever, John Haughey, in his well-known book, *Should Anyone Say Forever?* (1977), examined the components of commitment, the problems of and the justification for permanence, and answered "yes" to his own question. (See also Rene Voillaume, *Follow Me: The Call to Religious Life Today*, 1978.) The concept of collegiality as expounded by Vatican Council II was applied to the role of the religious superior in discussions on obedience. The shared responsibility of all members of the religious institute for the direction of the order was emphasized in Jean Galot's book *Inspiriter of the Community* earlier in the decade. While always holding the final authority, the superior has a particular role of "inspiriter," infusing life into the community, dialoging and discerning with the members, and providing for the spiritual and physical welfare of the community. Celibacy, the role of love in the lives of religious, received much attention in these years. Donald Goergen's *The Sexual Celibate* (1974), Christopher Kiesling's *Celibacy, Prayer and Friendship* (1978), Henri Nouwen's *Clowning in Rome* (1979), and Paul O'Connor's *Celibate Love* (1979) are representative of such works.

Authors continued to develop a theology of the religious life as in Juan Lozano, *Discipleship* (1980) and Francis Moloney, *Disciples and Prophets*, (1981). All of these books emphasized love as a positive foundational force in the life of a religious. Poverty was dealt with more extensively in the periodical literature and was always included in the general studies of the vows.

A noteworthy trend in publications after the Council was an emphasis on community development. Prior to the Council it was taken for granted that because religious lived together, worked and prayed together, there was a healthy community life. Because of changes in horarium, apostolic work, and adjustment to the needs of those for whom they worked, community life lost its appearance of external regularity. It was important to come to an understanding of what makes good community life beyond the externals of all members working, praying and being together at all times. Many works on community dealt with the topic from the spiritual viewpoint; e.g. Paul Hinnebusch, *Community in the Lord* (1975), K. Rahner, *Religious Life Today* (1976), David Knight, *Cloud by Day; Fire by Night* (1977), emphasizing community life as witness in the Church of the Lord's love. Religious communities held workshops and institutes on community living, studying it from the psychological, sociological, and theological points of view. Very interesting are the publications that discussed community life and communities as social entities. John Dondero and Thomas Frary, *New Pressures, New Responses in Religious Life* (Alba, 1979), focused on the human behavior which undergirds religious life. Charles Fracchia, *Living Together Alone* (Harper, 1979), reflected the interest of some in examining other religious groups outside the Western Christian monastic tradition. Along side the Catholic monasteries, he examined Buddhist, Quaker and Eastern communities, commenting on groups such as these as catalysts for change in the traditional Catholic communities. A book of particular use to those interested in the history of religious renewal in the Church was *Shaping the Coming Age of Religious Life* (Seabury, 1979) by Lawrence Cada, Raymond Fitz and several others. By exploring an historical and sociological model, the authors attempted to discover the underlying pattern and design of religious communities in order to inform present action and planning for the future. They viewed a community as a social entity subject to the normal life cycles of birth, growth and decline. Their idea of "refounding," or rebirthing as some have called it, at the decline phase of existence has assured some communities' survival throughout history. The failure to found anew explained the disappearance of orders in the past. By understanding this dynamic, the authors offered a process for revitalization or renewal in Catholic religious communities of the present. In *Climb along the Cutting Edge* (Paulist, 1977), several Benedictine sisters analyzed the process of change in religious orders and documented this change as it occurred in their own monasteries. Sister Joan Chittister noted in her preface to the book that they began this work "because history is slipping away from us"; thus, they saw the need to preserve a history of the process of renewal in its particular lived experience. The authors looked at convent life before and after the Council, the process of change in their monasteries, the role of the American Benedictine woman in the Catholic Church, the development of a theology of monasticism, and the personal effects of the change. An appendix provided the research instruments used in the study.

Retirement or preparation for it was not a common concern among religious until the recent past. Sisters who taught in the parochial schools frequently taught beyond the retirement age of sixty-five. As apostolates became more professionalized and greater concern was given to the development of the person, retirement became a reality or, more frequently, a change to a less physically demanding work. Periodical literature included articles on retirement from 1970. Catholic Hospital Association published Duschesne Herold's book *New Life; Preparation for Religious Retirement* (1973), which was primarily a how-to book, a resource for those charged with developing such programs for their communities. The appearance of this topic in the publica-

tions reveals a social, perhaps also an economic development among religious in recent years.

Pertinent to the psychological discussion of religious life
was the appearance of specialized programs for personal
development. These programs varied widely from personal
enrichment programs (e.g. Derham Community, St. Paul,
MN; Emmaus House, St. Louis, MO.) to therapeutic communities such as the House of Affirmation movement. The
House of Affirmation in Whitinsville, MA, publishes the
papers of its annual psycho-theological symposia. These
books, geared to clergy and religious, deal with issues of
emotional living in an age of stress. Each volume has
addressed a specific problem: *Coping* (1976), *Loneliness*
(1977), *Intimacy* (1978), *Belonging* (1979), *Guilt* (1980), and
Relationships (1982).

Somehow the lives of religious women have long been a
source of fascination to writers from all kinds of back-
grounds. This view "from the outside" gives another perspective of the life of the convent. Sara Harris interviewed
religious women of several different orders and, in *The
Sisters* (1970), recounted the changing world of the American nun. Her work accented orders that work among the
poor, described the lives of nuns before and after renewal,
and included a glimpse of the kind of woman who is in
orders today. Marcelle Bernstein, a non-Catholic journalist
of Jewish background, lived for four years with different
communities of sisters while she researched her book *The
Nuns* (1976). She interviewed sisters of Catholic and Protestant religious orders and found them very open to her
inquiries. Widely read, Bernstein quoted the Fathers of the
Church and Scripture passages pertinent to the religious
life. Both Harris and Bernstein treat the religious life in an
honest and sympathetic way. A somewhat different slant is
the work of a social anthropologist, Suzanne Campbell-
Jones, whose book *In Habit* (Pantheon, 1978) offered
insight into the history, daily life, and belief system of two
British orders, one a nursing order that had undergone little
change and the other a teaching order that had begun
changes as early as 1957. The book is a scholarly study

which, though British, has pertinence to a study of American religious orders.

Those who have left religious orders provide another perspective of religious life, most of them in contrast to the *Awful Disclosures* of an earlier age. Two examples will suffice. *The Courage to Choose: An American Nun's Story* (1975) by Mary Griffen captured very well the externals of the pre-Vatican II convent life. Griffen showed a certain affection for the life, saw some of its practical incongruities, and told them with humor. She had no ax to grind, and missed nothing in detailing the life. Helen Ebaugh's *Out of Cloister* (1977) was a sociological study that served as her dissertation. In her book, researched while still a community member, and written after she had left her order, Ebaugh presented a case study of three religious orders at different stages of change. The book was a thorough sociological study of organizational structures and the dilemmas that these organizations faced in terms of change. It contained statistical data on membership and studied decline in membership from a sociological perspective.

The topic of ex-nuns and departures from religion found in recent literature is indicative of a more open stance towards discussion of this formerly taboo subject. Charles Schleck discussed reasons given by those departing from religion and made suggestions to meet the situation (*Review for Religious*, "Departures from Religion," July 1968). By January, 1974, the Sacred Congregation of Religious issued a letter to religious orders (*Review for Religious*, July 1974) on the topic of assisting those who leave religious institutes. A sociological study by Lucinda San Giovanni, *Ex-Nuns* (1978), dealt with emergent role passages in adult life and based its findings on in-depth interviews with twenty ex-nuns who left in the late sixties and early seventies.

Another noteworthy trend in religious research is the appearance by the mid-seventies of dissertations on religious life. Earlier dissertations on the topic tended to be historical studies of an order — the foundation and/ or expansion of its works. A number of the recent dissertations studied effects of change in the orders; others studied religious commitment. Both the social sciences and theological studies are represented in these studies. (See Bibliography, Section 9.)

Not to be missed by the researcher of women's religious orders is the Sisters' Survey of 1980 done by Sister Marie Augusta Neal. This project was a follow-up to the Sisters' Survey of 1967 noted earlier in this essay. The 1967 survey was a population study as compared to the random sample survey of 1980. Thirty-one congregations were involved in 1980; twenty were invited to participate because of their location along a continuum of response to the religious belief scales of the 1967 survey. The other eleven responded voluntarily to a general invitation to all congregations through the Leadership Conference of Women Religious. Of the 428 items in the 1980 instrument, 175 were repeated from the original survey.

The 1980 survey was a response to the Call to Action letter of 1971 and its United States' implementation at the Detroit Conference of 1976 at which the Bishops set out recommendations for a program of social justice in the Catholic Church in the United States. The questions in the survey focused on how renewal in religious congregations of women have implemented the directives of Vatican Council II and post-conciliar papal documents. In her report (*Probe*, Vol. 10, May-June 1981, No. 5) Neal compared the findings of the 1980 survey with the results of 1967 on the sisters' response to the call for greater involvement of the Church with the poor and disadvantaged. The place of prayer in the lives of the sisters, the assessment of changes in structures, their hopes for the future development of religious orders, the sisters' views on changing apostolates are some of the areas compared. Results show, among other things, that morale in local communities of sisters is much higher, and that there is a high degree of participation in decision making in the orders. The sisters report better communication with administrators and greater sensitivity to needs of individual sisters. Noteworthy in the results is evidence of a continuing process of conversion as the sisters grapple with the gospel call for social justice, especially in work with and for the poor, with those marginalized by society, and with their personal response by a simple life style. Neal's final comment on her report (*Probe*, p. 7) summarized this on-going conversion well:

> The Survey indicates a great willingness of the Sisters of the United States to be part of the transforming action of the Church in the world. There is a real recognition that the poor of the world are central to that mission, but the number who are willing to listen specifically to the poor as they organize to claim their share of the world's goods and services to assure their survival... is still relatively small enough though the acceptance of that mission is relatively high... that God dwells with the poor in this transforming action is only on the very edge of our consciousness.... The challenge of that mission... is a conversion in process, but only just begun.

The report is very informative, the comparison with 1967 quite revealing. To be noted is that the conclusions of the survey are similar to the findings one gains from a survey of the literature — that external and organizational renewal has to a large extent been accomplished. On-going is the process of internal renewal, the call to a conversion to gospel values which will result in action.

A final and very important group of publications comes from several of the ten organizations of religious women in the United States. The most prominent and largest, the Leadership Conference of Women Religious (known as the Conference of Major Superiors of Women 1956-1971) is officially recognized by the Vatican and represents a majority of the religious women in this country. Several noteworthy volumes have been published by this association. *New Visions, New Roles* (1975) dealt with the role of women in the Church. *Widening the Dialogue* (1976), published jointly with the Canadian Religious Conference, presented the papers given during a summer seminar on Paul VI's *Evangelica Testificatio*. In 1976 the Leadership Conference identified "the articulation of a contemporary theology of religious life consonant with the call to penetrate the world with the Gospel message" as one of its long range goals. A questionnaire received from 520 religious women in the United States and the responses of those who analyzed the results formed the core of the work done by the Contemporary Theology Task Force. Hundreds of religious were involved in this study of the lived experience of religious women in the years since the Council. In 1979 LCWR published *Steps in the Journey* and a companion volume, *Resources for the Articulation of a Contemporary Theology of Religious Life*, both of them summaries of the process thus far. As a final phase in the project LCWR brought together six religious scholars, women and men, in a 1980 Writers Conference. From this phase resulted *Starting Points; Six Essays on the Experience of the United States Religious Women*, edited by Lora Quinonez. As it is titled, the book was intended to be a starting point, indicating that there is to be a continuance of the process. In 1979-1980 the Center for Applied Research in the Apostolate (CARA) conducted a survey relative to the experience of women in the Church as ministers and as ministered to. In February LCWR held a symposium to discuss the results of the survey and to make recommendations for the future. The proceedings of the symposium, published in *Women and Ministry: Present Experience and Future Hope* (1981), provide interesting and up-to-date information on the role and attitude of Catholic women in general and of religious women in particular. The Leadership Conference continues to develop a theology of religious life and to work for education for justice, including the furtherance of women's position in church and society.

In 1971 another group of religious superiors organized under the title of Consortium Perfectae Caritatis, now The Institute of Religious Life. This group has published the proceedings of its semi-annual general assemblies, representative of which are *The Religious Woman, Minister of Faith* (1974), *The Woman Religious — The Heart of the Church* (1975), *Sisters — Daughters of the Church Today* (1976), *Humanism, Christian or Secular* (1977) and *Increase Our Faith — Thoughts on Religious Life in Our Times* (1978).

These publications reveal a more conservative interpretation of renewal for religious. The speakers of these assemblies were more often male religious and members of the hierarchy as compared to the LCWR which has drawn to a greater extent on the expertise of theologians and other scholars among women religious.

A publication of interest is *Facets of the Future* (1976), which contained summaries of the papers given at a joint symposium sponsored by the Sister Formation Conference and CARA. Edited by Ruth McGoldrick and Cassian Yuhaus, the first section of the book focused on the future role of religious in the Church. A second section dealt with vocation and formation in religious community and on emerging ministries for religious. A final section made projections for "tomorrow."

The National Association of Women Religious (NAWR) published *Women in Ministry: A Sister's View* (1972), which reflected the changing status of women in society and consequently in religious orders, vis-a-vis ministry. Their periodical publication *Probe* keeps the membership abreast of Church and social issues especially as they relate to their objective of promoting a ministry of justice for women in the Church and in economic systems. Another group, the Black Sisters Conference, published *Black Religious Women as Part of the Answer* and *Black Catholic Commitment*, compiled by Sr. Elizabeth Harris. The latter publication featured accounts of black religious persons in the Detroit, Michigan, area in order to provide role models for black Catholics interested in religious life.

The development of organizations of religious women is an interesting phenomenon in itself, one which derives clearly from the renewal movement. Only the Conference of Major Superiors (LCWR, 1971) was organized before the Council. The remainder developed through the 1960s and 1970s to fulfill needs which individuals or groups felt were not met. The rise of these organizations is one indication of a developing consciousness among religious women of their role in the Church and in society. It reflects the changing social climate in which they arose. A complete list of these organizations, along with a brief history of each, is available in the annual *Catholic Almanac.*

Though not United States based, two other conferences of religious are pertinent to this discussion. In 1965, on the day that the Vatican Council closed, the International Union of Superiors General was formed. Their recent publication, *Religious Women Unafraid* (1979), consisted of reprints from the organization's Bulletins of 1975-1978. The articles, contributed by prominent religious women and men the world over, dealt with consecration and mission of religious women, the vows and the role of faith. Parallel to the Leadership Conference in the United States is the Candadian Religious Conference which represents both men and women religious of that country. Their *Donum Dei* series and their *Vita Evangelica* series deal with current trends of religious life. Many of the volumes are noteworthy, particularly *Religious Life: Tomorrow* (*Donum Dei,* No. 24, 1978) which contains proceedings of the Third Inter-American Meeting of Religious. The value of the book lies in the position papers contributed by the participating conferences (United States, Latin America and Canada) which give insight into the goals of these organizations.

Periodical Literature

Periodical literature in the late 70s and early 80s continued investigations of the many facets of religious life. The literature seems to indicate a better sense of direction in religious life. The externals of the life have changed and for the most part seem to be considered beyond question. Noteworthy are discussions on the quality of dedication and commitment of religious. Community life — its dynamics, its witness, quality of presence to one another, even its tensions — continues to be discussed in numerous articles. Articles on renewal, as such, seem to have peaked by the mid-70s. Articles on women, including the ordination of women, show a growing acceptance of the role of women in the institutional church and the development of feminine spirituality and ministry.

Several recent articles in *Review for Religious* are of importance to the researcher on religious life. George Aschenbrenner published a series of five annual articles dealing with trends and issues relative to religious. The first, "Currents in Spirituality: The Past Decade" (March 1980), presented a spiritual profile of the 70s, including in Part I the issues that affect the whole of society and in Part II these issues and others as they apply to religious and priests. The latter section dealt particularly with trends in understanding each of the vows, community life, and the relationship of religious to the institutional church. Aschenbrenner's second article, "Trends of 1980: Some Themes and a Few Specifics" (March 1981), dealt specifically with trends of the past year. He assumed the continuing trends noted in the first article and added four: concern for the possibility of a profound and faithful love; concern for a shared companionship in faith; concern for the paschal character; and concern for the quality of faith. In the third article of the series, "Trends and Issues in a Secularizing World" (March 1982), he noted ten trends and issues, among them the sacred-secular split, promotion of global and societal values, unity in diversity, women in church leadership and community aspects of religious life. He raised questions on current and past practices and made insightful comments on possible directions for the future.

Aschenbrenner's 1983 article on trends continued the basic theme of secularization presented in 1982. In "God for a Dark Journey" he dealt with "the spiritual struggle... to incarnate the life and love of God in a rapidly secularizing world." He noted two specific trends in present day religious life: 1) the rise of new religious groups which may or may not evolve into new forms of religious life and 2) the fact that there continues to be departures from religious orders. His 1984 article on trends, "Assessing and Choosing Even As the Journey Continues" (January 1984), points out that we are at "a special moment in our corporate pilgrimage." It is time to evaluate the past twenty years of experimentation, though not a time to discontinue development. In the con-

text of the recent document on religious life and the new
code of Canon Law, he discusses the need for public witness
of religious, the living of the vows of obedience and poverty,
the diversification of apostolic works, and the lack of vocations to religious orders. Aschenbrenner's five articles provide the reader with thought-provoking considerations
regarding the movements current in religious life of the 80s.

Two other articles are noteworthy. Juan Lozano's excellent article, "Trends in Religious Life Today" (July 1983),
discusses ideas similar to those of Aschenbrenner under
headings of the centrality of the person, emancipation of
women, life over institutions, openness to the world, and
reinterpretation of religious life. Lozano ends by raising the
possibility that the religious life of the future will be that of a
prophetic miniority requiring different qualifications for
those entering. In briefer form, Stephen Tutas reiterated
many of the same ideas in his "Signs of Hope in Religious
Life Today" (January 1983).

The researcher will find several other magazines useful,
among them *Sisters Today*, mentioned earlier in this essay.
Edited by Benedictine men until fall, 1979, it is now under
the management of Benedictine women who have retained
the purpose of the magazine set out in the 1960s, "to explore
the role of the religious woman in the Church in our time."
The articles deal with many of the same topics as *Review for
Religious*, though they are generally shorter and more popular in style. As a journal written over some thirty years
specifically for religious women, it gives insight into the
kind of literature, along with the *Review*, that has been
available for sisters during this period of renewal.

The magazine *Origins*, the National Catholic News Service letter, has also carried articles on renewal of religious
life from time to time. *The Pope Speaks* provides the
researcher with an on-going source for publications from
Rome, although these in the recent past have been systematically presented in the *Review for Religious* as well. Other
journals, such as *Spiritual Life* and *Spirituality Today*, deal
primarily with topics related to the spiritual life.

Chapter Four

REFLECTIONS

The recent renewal in religious life dates from 1950 when Pius XII and the Sacred Congregation began meeting with religious superiors. The Vatican Council, 1962-1965, articulated this renewal for the large audience of religious. During the sixties the social climate of change provided the broad framework for the movement. Within the Church such concepts as the universal call to holiness and collegiality explicated by the Council placed the responsibility for renewal on all Christians and in particular on each individual religious.

The ensuing years have been years of questions, of doubts, of examination and search. Old forms have crumbled or become inoperative and new ones are not completely in place. By the 1980's some trends are apparent in the publications on religious; among them is a clear indication of women religious taking responsibility for their own lives and for the development of the future of religious life. Especially encouraging is the presence of women religious writers, the quality of whose writing attests to the wisdom of an earlier movement which encouraged higher education for religious women, especially in the field of theology. The publications on religious life reflect the concern for the person in their emphasis on the importance of the development of the feminine religious personality in its psychological, spiritual and apostolic dimensions. Religious orders have come to realize that this fullness of religious womanhood is their chief asset in the realization of their apostolic mission. This concern of religious has come to include improvement of women's position in the larger society and in the Church. Convinced of the special contribution which women can make, religious women have expessed solidarity with other women in seeking opportunities denied them both in the Church and in society.

The renewal of religious life is very much tied to the emergence of the laity's more active participation in the Church. Together these two groups, religious women and laity, are asking for a greater voice, for more direct sharing in the spiritual life and apostolic ministry of the People of God. As the laity continue to participate in new ways in the apostolic, liturgical and spiritual life of the Church, it is possible that some will ask for a deepening of this experience through new forms of religious life. Already we have seen community forms develop around the marriage encounter movement, the TEC retreat, the charismatic forms of prayer, and the lay associates of established religious orders. Just as secular institutes earlier in this century responded to a new spiritual and apostolic need in the life of the Church, new needs may give rise to new forms of religious life alongside the celibate communal organization as we know it today. It is probably true that in the future the number of members in the celibate communal religious orders will be considerably smaller than in the recent past. It is possible also that the pluralism characteristic of contemporary American society may show itself in the Church in the development of multiple options for those interested in religious life. The celibate communal form will undoubtedly be one of the options.

While the shortage in vocations is decried in most of the publications of the past decade, it is apparent that this crisis was the catalyst that helped bring about the sharing of apostolic works with the laity. Even with fewer members religious communities have gradually moved into a diversity of new apostolic works, especially those pertaining to social justice and global values, made possible in large part by this cooperation with the laity. Noteworthy in the publications on vocation in the late seventies is a change in emphasis from discussion of the shortage of vocations to a position of the need to enrich and deepen collaboration with laity in the works of the Church.

To be a religious woman today is not as popular a life profession as it was at the beginning of the era under discussion. "Why do they stay?" is asked at least as often as the earlier question, "Why do they leave?" The changes in religious life are truly a challenge that by and large has been accepted by religious women. The need for continuing this renewal is apparent in the literature, lest religious life return to the stagnated state in which it found itself in the fifties. The challenge of religious today is to be involved in the world and at the same time to stand away from it, to call religious and others to respond to the Christian message to build the Kingdom of God on earth. The publications of the recent past on religious life emphasize much more the need to be authentic religious persons than to fear being "secularized" by involvement in the world. The trend in the publications to explicate a theology of religious life reveals the direction of a deepened understanding and response to the documents of Vatican II and even more so to the teachings of Jesus in the Gospels as they pertain to community life and the apostolates of the future.

Nor is there complete unanimity among religious women, or even their leaders, on the meaning and pratice of renewal. The literature reveals a wide scope of interpretation and application of the Church's directives for renewal. Serious publications of the late seventies and early eighties contain less of this controversy than was found in the sixties, even though current popular publications occasionally contain a criticism of developments in religious orders and call for a return to the old forms.

Since the mid-seventies there is evidence that we have

come to reflect more frequently on religious life through the disciplines of social history and sociology, to stand aside and look at what has happened and is happening, to describe the religious life of the past, to record the changes and the process of these changes, and to analyze the new directions religious life is now taking. Such writings by religious and non-religious, both Catholic and non-Catholic, seem to herald the end of an era and the beginning of a new paradigm in the lived expression of religious life in the Church. Recent Ph. D. dissertations on such topics as social organization of religious orders, on acceptance of change by religious as a group and as individuals, and comparative studies on celibacy, sexuality and the meaning of life between religious and lay women, done both in private and public institutions, may be another indication of the end of an era in religious life. This is not to say that religious life will no longer be part of the Church's future. Rather, it means that we have come to the end of a phase in communal celibate orders marked by strong institutionalization and are entering a new paradigm characterized by greater concern for the individual and an attempt to achieve a greater balance of individual and community values.

The movement to establish archives in religious orders and to make possible the use of these archives by the public (e.g. Evangeline Thomas, *Guide to Religious Archives of the U.S.,* Bowker, 1982) opened an area of knowledge to the researcher which once was clearly marked "Cloister" or "For Religious Only." Articles such as Aschenbrenner's and Lozano's which analyze trends in religious life also indicate that we are assessing the present as we move into the future.

Perhaps the clearest indication that we have come to the end of an era and are moving into a new phase is the statement by Pope John Paul II that the period of experimentation is over with the publication of the revised code of canon law (Letter to Bishops, April 3, 1983). The promulgation of this code of law on January 25, 1983 culminated more than twenty years of work begun by Vatican Council II. In Book II: The People of God, the Code deals with legislation concerning consecrated life in the Church in all its present forms: religious institutes, secular institutes and societies of apostolic life. The most immediately apparent difference of this code from that of 1918 is that there are 173 canons or laws pertaining to religious and religious life in contrast to some 2000 in the earlier code. Also obvious from a cursory reading is that, in the revised code, many particulars of the life are left to regulation by the individual congregations. The section on religious life in the 1918 code dealt very much with external regulation, devoting a large part to the role of authority in the life of the religious. Other than stating in Canon 487 that religious observe the evangelical counsels of obedience, chastity, and poverty, the 1918 code goes no further to define the basic concept of these counsels.

Of necessity any code must define the legal and juridical aspects of life in a religious institute. However, the revised code presents religious life more directly as a following of Jesus and a dedication to God in service for the Kingdom. The concepts basic to the vows and community life are strikingly in contrast with those of the earlier code, and are perhaps an expression of, or key to, some of the more significant changes in religious life since Vatican II. Very briefly, the revised code presents chastity as "embraced for the sake of the Kingdom of heaven, a sign of the world to come and a source of greater fruitfulness in an undivided heart." Poverty is defined as the "imitation of Christ who was for our sake made poor when he was rich," and obedience is "undertaken in the spirit of faith and love in the following of Christ who was obedient unto death."(Canons 599,600,601). Community life according to the revised code "is to be an example of universal reconciliation in Christ" and should be a source of mutual assistance to fulfill one's vocation. (c. 602)

One comes away from a perusal of the literature from 1950 to 1983 with a feeling of optimism because apparent in the literature is a continuing deepening of our understanding of the meaning of consecration and the call to commitment and discipleship. There is evident not only a response to the call of the Church for renewal, but especially a response to the call of Jesus in the Gospels to build the kingdom of God on earth. The living of this dual challenge in the context of contemporary society will continue to be the source of continuing renewal for religious.

Chapter Five

ON THE STUDY OF CHANGE
IN RELIGIOUS ORDERS

Included here are suggestions for further research and a bibliography of materials on renewal in religious orders since 1950. Like the essay, the bibliography is limited to religious women in active orders. Male religious and contemplative orders were excluded from this survey because their experience of renewal, though related, is somewhat different from that of active orders of women.

The bibliography contains only a representative selection of the published works available to the researcher. Research on renewal of orders will necessitate the use of other materials, primary and secondary, as suggested by the particular topic. The archives of individual religious orders and the archives of dioceses should not be neglected where pertinent. A very obvious important source is to be found in those women who have lived religious life during the past thirty-five years. Most topics will necessitate discussion of the trends in the total church during the time under discussion.

Recent dissertations on religious women reveal a renewed interest in this subject. The topic offers possibilities of research in many disciplines: theology, religious history, social history, sociology, and psychology, to name a few. The study of religious life as a social institution could become productive for the population at large to achieve a better understanding of religious women and their participation in the larger society. Studying the orders as social institutions can also be a valuable source for the orders themselves and enable them to come to a better understanding of themselves as a social group. One must bear in mind that the religious dimension and motivation of persons living this life are important factors, especially when studying religious life as a social institution.

Anyone interested in studying religious orders will find an almost unmined field of research with many possibilities. American Catholic sisterhoods are a well defined group of sufficient size and homogeneity to facilitate the study. The following are some suggested areas of research:

1. The experience of change in a particular religious order; attitudes toward and understanding of the change by the members; attitudes toward the future of the order.

2. The change in interpretation of the vows (celibacy, obedience and poverty) and community life: in the documents from the Pope and the Sacred Congregation; in the Constitution or Rule of a given order or orders; in the mind of individual members; in the practice of the vows and community life.

3. The change in the place or role of religious women in the Church in relation to society, and how religious relate to hierarchy, to clergy and to laity.

4. Religious women and the women's movement: exposure of religious women to women's issues; perception of and attitudes of religious towards the women's movement. (See E. Kolmer, "Religious Women and the Women's Movement," in Janet James, ed., *Women in American Religion*, University of Pennsylvania Press, 1980).

5. The image of religious women in the media: popular literature, film, television; how this image has changed since 1950.

6. Changes in institutional, organization structures of religious orders, the underlying motivation and forces which effected these changes, understanding of the members of the reasons for these changes.

7. Comparative study of the perceptions of those who have left religious life and those who remain regarding selected aspects of the life. See National Sisters Conference study by Modde and Koval on departures from religious women's communities between 1965-1972, Summary, *Catholic Almanac*, 1974, p. 570.

8. Perception of and attitudes toward the future of religious life: by those in the orders; by those outside the orders. One might study an order, or several orders, in terms of L. Cada and R. Fitz's historic-sociological model of the life span of institutions.

9. What might account for the different "personalities" of religious orders? Ways in which the "personality" of an order effects the process of change in an order. Ways in which the "personality" of an order might change or not change as a result of the recent change in religious orders.

10. Works or apostolates of religious women, traditional and new. The change in apostolic works from teaching and nursing to working with prisoners, with the aged, with abused women and children. The changing role of the sister even in the traditional apostolates.

11. The beginnings and development of organizations of religious women — the social, sociological and psychological pressures out of which they rose.

As we have seen, changes in religious life since 1950, and particularly since the Council, have been large scale in a short period of time. The changes of clothing and life style are the externals noted most easily. Other changes, e.g. those related to the interpretation of vows, the place of sisters in Church and society, the question of the "proper" apostolic works for sisters reveal a deeper renewal of sisterhoods in the Church. The externals of clothing and life style are not unrelated; in fact they are an integral part of the underlying concepts from which these changes arose. A study of changes in religious life in the recent past can reveal how, even though essential elements of a social institution remain the same, there is much in the practice and life of such an institution that can be adapted to a changing larger social milieu. Study of the changes in religious orders will further understanding of changes in the Church as well. The suggested topics listed above in no way exhaust the possible topics of research. Perusal of the literature and acquaintance with the topic will suggest further topics.

BIBLIOGRAPHY ON RENEWAL OF RELIGIOUS ORDERS OF WOMEN

1. PAPAL AND ROMAN DOCUMENTS

Benedictine Monks of Solesmes. *The States of Perfection.* Papal Teachings. St. Paul's Editions, 1967. Documents from Pope Benedict XIV to John XXIII.

Daughters of St. Paul. *Documents on Renewal for Religious.* St. Paul's Editions, 1974. Contains documents from John XXIII, from Sacred Congregation, from Vatican Council, from Paul VI.

Daughters of St. Paul. *Religious Life in the Light of Vatican II.* St. Paul's Editions, 1967. Includes selected documents on renewal and brief commentaries. Includes directives on updating constitutions.

Courtois, Gaston. *The States of Perfection.* Papal documents from Leo XII to Pius XII. Westminster: Newman Press, 1961.

John Paul II. *Faithfulness to the Gospel.* St. Paul's Editions, 1982.

John Paul II. *Visible Signs of the Gospel.* St. Paul's Editions, 1980.

Paul VI. *Address to All Religious.* May 23, 1964. National Catholic Welfare Conference, 1964.

Paul VI. *Ecclesiae Sanctae.* Apostolic letter issued on Norms implementing Four Decrees of Vatican II. August 6, 1966.

Paul VI. *Evangelica Testificatio.* Apostolic Exhortation on Renewal of Religious Life, 1971.

Paul VI. *Renovationis Causam.* Instruction of the Sacred Congregation for Religious and Secular Institutes. January 6, 1969. On Renewal of Religious Formation.

Paul VI. *Fidelity and Relevance.* Talks of Paul VI. Boston, 1970.

Paul VI. *Perfectae Caritatis. The Decree on the Adaptation and Renewal of the Religious Life.* October 28, 1965.

Paul VI. *Address to Nuns.* May 16, 1966. To the Fourteenth General Conference of the Union of Major Superiors of Italy. National Catholic Conference, 1966.

Pius XII. *Address of His Holiness to Congress of Religious.* December 8, 1950. Rome, 1950.

Pius XII. *Allocution to the Superiors General of Female Institutes and Congregations.* September 15, 1952.

Pius XII. *Discourse to Teaching Sisters.* September 13, 1951. See Courtois, *States of Perfection.*

Pius XII. *Letter* to Cardinal Micara on Adaptation of Religious to Contemporary Conditions. November 12, 1950. See Courtois.

Pius XII. *Sacra Virginitas. On Christian Virginity.* March 25, 1954.

Pius XII. *Sponsa Christi.* November 21, 1950.

Pius XII. *The States of Perfection.* Second General Congress December 12, 1957. National Catholic Conference, 1957.

Sacred Congregation of Religious. *Consecrated Life.* The Holy See Speaks to Religious and Members of Secular Institutes. Vol. 1. No. 1. Institute on Religious Life, 1976.

Sacred Congregation of Religious. *Religious and Human Promotion.* April 25-28, 1978. St. Paul's Editions. 1980.

Sacred Congregation of Religious. *The Contemplative Dimension of Religious Life.* March 1980. St. Paul's Editions, 1980.

Sacred Congregation of Religious. *Instruction to the Superiors of Religious Communities on the Careful Selection and Training of Candidates for the States of Perfection and Sacred Orders.* Rome. 1961.

Sacred Congregation of Religious. *Essential Elements of the Religious Life.* Rome, 1983.

Vatican Council II. *Religious Life — A Mystery in Christ and the Church.* A Collated Study According to Vatican Council II and Subsequent Papal and Ecclesiastical Documents. Rose Eileen Masterson, editor. Alba House, 1975.

Vatican Council II. *The Religious Life Defined.* An Official Commentary on the Deliberations of the Second Vatican Council. Ralph Wiltgen, Editor. Techny, 1970.

2. RENEWAL OF RELIGIOUS ORDERS

Alberione, Giacomo. *Insight Into Religious Life.* Boston, St. Paul's, 1977.

Barwig, Regis. *Changing Habits.* New York: Pageant Press, 1970.

Berkery, Patrick. *Restructuring Religious Life. A Plan for Renewal.* Alba House, 1968.

Beyer, Jean Baptiste. *Religious Life or Secular Institute.* Rome: Gregorian Press, 1970.

Bland, Joan. *The Pastoral Vision of John Paul II.* Chicago: Franciscan Herald Press, 1982.

Bloesch, Donald. *Wellsprings of Renewal. Promise in Christian Communal Life.* Eerdmans, 1974.

Cada, Lawrence and Raymond Fitz, et. al. *Shaping the Coming Age of Religious Life.* Seabury Press, 1979.

Canadian Religious Conference. *Religious Life Tomorrow.* Ottawa, 1978.

Chittister, Joan. *Climb Along the Cutting Edge. Analysis of Change in Religious Life.* Paulist Press, 1977.

Clarke, Thomas. *New Pentecost or New Passion. Direction of Religious Life Today.* Paulist Press, 1973.

Collins, Leonard. *Proceedings of the Sisters' Institute of Spirituality.* 1954, 1955, 1956. South Bend: University of Notre Dame Press.

Consortium Perfectae Caritatis. *Humanism—Christian or Secular. The Evangelical Life in the Living Church.* Proceedings of the Twelfth and Thirteenth General Assemblies of the Consortium., 1977.

Consortium Perfectae Caritatis. *Increase Our Faith—Thoughts on Religious Life of Our Times.* Proceedings of the Fourteenth and Fifteenth General Assemblies., 1978.

Consortium Perfectae Caritatis. *Sisters, Daughters of the Church Today.* Proceedings of the Tenth and Eleventh General Assemblies of the Consortium., 1976.

Consortium Perfectae Caritatis. *The Woman Religious— Heart of the Church.* A Compilation of Addresses given at the Ninth General Assembly. Boston, St. Paul's 1975.

Dubay, Thomas. *Can Religious Life Survive?* Dimension Books, 1973.

Dyer, Ralph. *The New Religious.* Milwaukee: Bruce Publishers, 1967.

Faricy, Robert, *The End of Religious Life.* Winston Press, 1983.

Gaiani, P. Vitus. *For a Better Religious Life.* St. Paul's Editions, 1962.

Gallen, Joseph. *Canon Law for Religious: An Explanation.* New York: Alba House, 1983.

Gambari, Elio. *Renewal in Religious Life.* General Principles, Constitutions, Formation. St. Paul's Editions, 1967.

Garrone, Gabriel. *The Nun. Sacrament of God's Saving Presence.* Alba House, 1967.

Gelpi, Donald. *Discerning the Spirit. Foundations and Futures of Religious Life.* Sheed and Ward, 1970.

Gelpi, Donald. *Functional Asceticism. A Guideline for American Religious.* Sheed and Ward, 1966.

Gleason, Robert. *The Restless Religious.* Dayton: Pflaum, 1968.

Grollmes, Eugene. *Vows But No Walls. An Analysis of Religious Life.* St. Louis: Herder, 1967.

Haley, Joseph. *The Sister in America Today.* South Bend: University of Notre Dame Press, 1965.

Haley, Joseph. *Proceedings of the Sisters' Institute of Spirituality,* 1953, 1957, 1958, 1959. South Bend: University of Notre Dame Press.

Fanfani, Ludovici and Kevin O'Rourke. *Canon Law for Religious Women.* Priory Press, 1961.

Gambari, Elio. *Religious Women and Canon Law.* Philadelphia: The Peter Reilly Co., 1960. Institute of Spirituality for Women Religious, Philadelphia, August, 1958.

Hardon, John A. *Religious Life Today.* Boston, St. Paul's, 1977.

Haughey, John. *Should Anyone Say Forever? On Making, Keeping and Breaking Commitments.* Doubleday, Image Books, 1977.

Herold, Duschesne. *New Life: Preparation of Religious for Retirement.* St. Louis: Catholic Hospital Association, 1973.

Hinnebusch, Paul. *The Signs of the Times and the Religious Life*. Sheed, 1967.

Hogan, William. *No Race Apart. Religious Life in the Mystical Body*. Holy Cross Press, 1966.

Hudon, Rosemarie. *Nuns: Community Prayer and Change*. Alba House, 1966.

Huizing, Peter and William Basset. *The Future of Religious Life*. Seabury Press, 1975.

Huyghe, Gerard. (ed.) *Religious Orders in the Modern World*. Newman Press, 1965.

Huyghe, Gerard. *Tensions and Change. The Problems of Religious Orders Today*. Newman Press, 1966.

International Union of Superiors General. *Women Religious Unafraid*. Select Reprints, 1975-1978. Asian Trading Corporation. 1979.

Kelly, Gerald. *Guidance for Religious*. Newman Press, 1956.

Kopp, Lillanna. *Sudden Spring Sixth Stage Sisters*. Sunspot Publications, 1979.

Leadership Conference of Women Religious (with the Canadian Religious Conference). *Widening the Dialogue*. Reflections on "Evangelica Testificatio," 1976.

Lovasik, Lawrence. *The Sister for Today*. Meditation on the Religious Life in the Spirit of Pius XII, John XXIII, Paul VI and Vatican Council II. Marian Action Publications, 1965.

McGoldrick, Ruth, and Cassian Yuhaus. *Facets of the Future of Religious Life, USA*. Our Sunday Visitor, 1976.

McKenna, Lawrence. *Women of the Church*. Kenedy, 1967.

Mary Edna, Sister. *The Religious Life*. Penguin, 1968.

Meyers, Sr. Bertrande. *Sisters for the 21st Century.* Sheed, 1965.

Modde, Margaret Mary. *Manual for Writing New Constitutions for Institutions of the Consecrated Life.* 1979.

Muckenhirn, Sr. Charles Borromeo, (ed.) *The Changing Sister.* Notre Dame: Fides Book, 1965.

Muckenhirn, Sr. Charles Borromeo. *Implications for Renewal.* Notre Dame Press, 1967.

Muckenhirn, Sr. Charles Borromeo. *The New Nuns.* New American Library, 1967.

Murphy-O'Connor, Jerome. *What is Religious Life? A Critical Appraisal.* M. Glazier, Inc. 1977.

National Congress of Religious in the United States. Proceedings. *Religious Community Life in the United States.* Paulist Press, 1952.

National Congress of Religious of the United States. *Religious Life in the Church Today. Prospect and Retrospect.* Proceedings of the Women's Section of the Second National Congress of Religious in the United States. Notre Dame Press, 1961.

O'Leary, Mary Florence Margaret. *Our Time is Now. A Study of Some Modern Congregations and Secular Institutes.* Newman Press, 1956.

O'Reilly, James. *Lay and Religious States of Life: Their Distinction and Complementarity.* Chicago: Franciscan Herald Press, 1976.

O'Reilly, John. *Voices of Change.* St. Louis: Herder and Co., 1970.

O'Rourke, Kevin. *Reflections on Renewal.* Chicago: Cross and Crown Publications, 1970.

O'Rourke, Kevin, ed. *Religious Life in the 70's.* Dubuque, Iowa: Aquinas Institute of Theology.

Pelton, Robert. *Proceedings.* Institute for Local Superiors, 1962, 1963. University of Notre Dame Press, 1963, 1964.

Perinelle, Joseph. *God's Highways: The Religious Life and Secular Institutes.* Blackfriars, 1958.

Predovich, Nicholas. *The Challenge of "Radical" Renewal.* Alba House, 1968.

Regamy, Raymond. *Renewal in the Spirit: Rediscovering the Religious Life.* Boston: St. Paul's, 1980.

Religious Sisters. English Version of *Directory of Superiors and Adaptation of Religious Life.* Newman Press, 1958.

Renard, A. C. *The Nun in the Modern World.* New York: Herder and Herder, 1961.

Renard, Alexander. *The New Spirit in the Convent.* Dimension Books, 1968.

Romb, Anselm W. *Signs of Contradiction: Religious Life in a Time of Change.* St. Louis: B. Herder, 1967.

Review For Religious. *Questions on Religious Life.* St. Mary's, Kansas, 1964.

Schlitzer, Albert. *Proceedings.* The Institute for Local Superiors, 1964, 1965, 1966. University of Notre Dame Press, 1965, 1966, 1967.

Sisters of Charity of BVM. *The Problems That Unite Us.* Proceedings of Institute July 31 — August 20, 1965. Chicago: Mt. Carmel, 1965.

Sisters of Mercy of the Union. *Commitment in a Changing World.* 1973.

Smith, Hilary. *Realism in Renewal.* Techny, 1969.

Suenens, Joseph. *The Nun in the World.* Newman Press, 1963.

Tate, Judith. *Sisters for the World.* Herder and Herder, 1965.

Tate, Judith. *Religious Women.* Herder and Herder, 1970.

Theological Institute for Local Superiors. *Adaptation of the Religious Life to Modern Conditions.* Notre Dame Press, 1961.

Theological Institute for Local Superiors. *Apostolic Dimensions of the Religious Life.* Notre Dame Press, 1966.

Theological Institute for Local Superiors. *Dimensions of Authority in the Religious Life.* Notre Dame Press, 1966.

Valentine, Sr. M. Hester, *Prayer and Renewal.* Proceedings and Communications of Regional Meetings of the Sister Formation Conferences, 1969. Fordham University Press, 1970.

3. VOWS AND COMMUNITY

Beha, Helen Marie. *The Dynamics of Community.* New York: Corpus Books, 1970.

Beha, Helen Marie. *Living Community.* Milwaukee: Bruce Publishing Co. 1967.

Carpentier, Rene. *Life in the City of God. An Introduction to the Religious Life.* Translated by John Joyce. Benziger Bros., 1959.

Corstanje, Austpicus. *The Covenant of God's Poor. On the Biblical Interpretation of the Testament of St. Francis Assisi.* Franciscan Herald Press, 1966.

Cary-Elwes, Columba. *Law, Liberty and Love, A Study in Christian Obedience.* London, 1950.

Center for Applied Research in the Apostolate. *A Practical Approach to Community.* 1967.

Carroll, L. Patrick. *To Love, to Share, to Serve.* Liturgical Press, 1979.

Connor, Paul. *Celibate Love.* Huntington: Our Sunday Visitor, 1979.

Cussianovich, Alejandro. *Religious Life and the Poor. Liberation Theology Perspectives.* Maryknoll: Orbis Books, 1979.

Dondero, John P. and Thomas P. Frary. *New Pressures, New Responses in Religious Life.* Alba House, 1979.

Dion, Philip. *Sister's Vow of Chastity.* New York: Wagner, 1965.

Fracchia, Charles. *Living Together Alone.* New York: Harper and Row, 1979.

Galot, Jean. *Inspiriter of the Community. The New Role of the Religious Superior.* Alba House, 1971.

Georgen, Donald. *The Sexual Celibate.* Seabury, 1974.

Hinnebusch, Paul. *Community in the Lord.* Notre Dame: Ave Maria Press, 1975.

Heijke, John. *An Ecumenical Light on the Renewal of Religious Community Life.* Taize. Duquesne University Press, 1967.

Kiesling, Christopher. *Celibacy, Prayer and Friendship.* Alba House, 1978.

Kean, Claude. *As One of them.* Letters to a Sister Superior. Newman Press, 1965.

Leclerq, Jacques. *The Religious Vocation.* P. J. Kenedy, 1955.

Leeming, Bernard. *The Mysticism of Obedience.* St. Paul's Editions, 1964.

LeGrand, Lucien. *The Biblical Doctrine of Virginity.* New York: Sheed and Ward, 1963.

McGoldrick, Desmond. *Independence Through Submission.* Pittsburgh: Duquesne University Press, 1964.

Meissner, William. *Assault on Authority.* Maryknoll: Orbis Books, 1971.

Moran, Gabriel and Maria Harris. *Experiences in Community. Should Religious Life Survive?* New York: Herder and Herder, 1968.

Moran, Gabriel. *The New Community. Religious Life in an Era of Change.* Herder and Herder, 1970.

Nouwen, Henri. *Clowning in Rome. Reflections on Solitude, Celibacy, Prayer and Contemplation.* Image Books, 1979.

O'Doherty, Eamonn. *Vocation, Formation, Consecration and Vows. Theological and Psychological Considerations.* Alba House, 1971.

Religious Life Series. *Chastity.* London: Blackfriars, 1955.

Religious Life Series. *Communal Life.* Newman Press, 1957.

Religious Life Series. *Poverty.* Newman Press, 1954.

Ronsin, F. X. *To Govern is to Love.* New York: Society of St. Paul, 1955.

Theological Institute for Local Superiors. *The Vows and Perfection.* Notre Dame Press, 1962.

The Way. Poverty. Supplement. Spring, 1970.

Valentine, Ferdinand. *All For the King's Delight. A Treatise on Christian Chastity Principally for Religious Sisters.* Newman Press, 1958.

Valentine, Ferdinand. *Religious Obedience.* Newman Press, 1952.

Van der Poel, Cornelius. *Religious Life: A Risk of Love.* Dimension Books, 1972.

Watterott, Ignaz. *Guidance of Religious. Considerations on the Duties of Religious Superiors.* St. Louis: Herder, 1950.

4. SPIRITUALITY; THEOLOGY OF RELIGIOUS LIFE

Alberione, Giacomo. *Religious Life: Life of Courageous Souls.* Meditations and Conferences. Boston: St. Paul's, 1957.

Biskupek, Aloysius. *Conferences on the Religious Life.* Milwaukee: Bruce Pub., 1957.

Blocker, Hyacinth. *Good Morning, Good People. Reflections on the Spiritual Life.* Cincinnati, 1954.

Canadian Conference of Religious. *The Prophetic Role of Religious.* Ottawa, 1977.

Colin, Louis. *Striving for Perfection. The Fundamental Obligation of the Religious State.* Newman Press, 1956.

Dodd, Francis. *Spiritual Conferences.* Emmitsburg: St. Joseph Press, 1959.

Doyle, Charles H. *Leaven of Holiness: Conferences for Religious.* Newman Press, 1955.

Doyle, Charles H. *Little Steps to Great Holiness.* Newman Press, 1956.

Doyle, Stephen. *Covenant Renewal in Religious Life.* Biblical Reflections. Franciscan Herald, 1975.

Dubay, Thomas. *Dawn of a Consecration. Meditations for Young Sisters.* Boston: St. Paul's, 1964.

Dubay, Thomas. *Ecclesial Women. Towards a Theology of the Religious State.* Alba House, 1970.

Duffey, Felix. *With Anxious Care.* St. Louis: Herder, 1961.

Faricy, Robert L. *Spirituality for Religious Life.* Paulist Press, 1976.

Farrell, Edward. *The Theology of Religious Vocation.* St. Louis: Herder, 1951.

Gambari, Elio. *The Global Mystery of Religious Life.* St. Paul's Editions, 1970.

Gambari, Elio. *Unfolding the Mystery of Religious Life.* Boston: St. Paul's, 1973.

Gleason, Robert. *To Live is Christ. Nature and Grace in the Religious Life.* Sheed and Ward, 1961.

Guardini, Romano. *Prayer in Practice.* Pantheon Books, 1957.

Hagspiel, Bruno. *Convent Readings and Reflections.* Milwaukee: Bruce Publishing Co., 1959.

Hagspiel, Bruno. *Spiritual Highlights for Sisters.* Milwaukee: Bruce, 1960.

Haring, Bernard. *Acting on the Word.* New York: Farrar, Strauss, 1968.

Hinnebusch, Paul. *Religious Life, A Living Liturgy.* Sheed, 1965.

Herbst, Winifred. *The Question Box for Sisters.* New York: St. Paul, 1961.

Herbst, Winifred. *The Sisters Want to Know.* Liturgical Press, 1958.

Herbst, Winifred. *The Sisters Are Asking.* Newman Press, 1956.

Hoeger, Frederick T. *The Convent Mirror. A Series of Conferences for Religious.* New York: Pustet, 1951.

Jeanne d'Arc, Sister. *Witness and Consecration.* Translated by Marie Bourgier. Priory Press, 1966.

Kelleher, Sean B. *A Biblical Approach to Religious Life.* Asian Trading Corporation, 1979.

Klimisch, S. Mary Jane. *The One Bride. The Church and Consecrated Virginity.* Sheed and Ward, 1965.

Knight, David M. *Cloud by Day; Fire by Night. The Religious Life as Passionate Response to God.* Asian Trading Corporation, 1977.

Lavaud, Benoit. *The Meaning of the Religious Life.* Newman Press, 1955.

Mary Laurence, Sister. *One Nun to Another.* Newman Press, 1954.

Leclerq, Jean. *The Life of Perfection. Points of View on the Essence of the Religious State.* Collegeville, 1961.

Leen, Edward. *Retreat Notes for Religious.* Kenedy, 1959.

Lozano, Juan M. *Discipleship. Toward an Understanding of Religious Life.* Chicago: Claret Center for Resources in Spirituality, 1980.

Martelet, Gustav. *The Church's Holiness and Religious Life.* Review for Religious, 1966.

Metz, Johannes. *Followers of Christ. The Religious Life and the Church.* Paulist Press, 1978.

Moffat, John E. *Listen, Sister Superior.* McMullen, 1953.

Moffat, John E. *Look, Sister.* McMullen, 1956.

Moloney, Francis. *Disciples and Prophets: A Biblical Model for the Religious Life.* New York: Crossroads, 1981.

Murphy, John F. *The Virtues on Parade.* Milwaukee: Bruce Publishers, 1959.

Nash, Robert. *The Nun at Her Priedieu.* Newman Press, 1955.

O'Grady, Colm. *The Challenge to Religious Life Today.* London: Geoffrey Chapman, 1970.

O'Meara, Thomas. *Holiness and Radicalism in Religious Life.* New York: Herder and Herder, 1970.

Orsy, Ladislaus. *Open to the Spirit. Religious Life after Vatican II.* Washington, 1968.

Quinonez, Lora Ann. *Starting Points. Six Essays Based on the Experience of United States Women Religious.* Leadership Conference of Women Religious, Washington, D.C., 1980.

Rahner, Karl. *The Religious Life Today*. Seabury Press, 1976.

Religious Life Series. *The Doctrinal Instruction of Religious Sisters*. Newman Press, 1956.

Stanley, David. *Faith and Religious Life. A New Testament Perspective*. Paulist Press, 1971.

Theological Institute for Local Superiors. *Prayer and Sacrifice*. Notre Dame Press, 1962.

Tillard, J. N. *The Mystery of Religious Life*. R. F. Smith, editor. St. Louis: Herder, 1967.

Victorine, Sister. *Christlikeness. Conferences for Religious on Spiritual Transformation through a Christocentric Life*. Newman Press, 1951.

Watterott, Ignaz. *Religious Life and the Spirit*. St. Louis: Herder, 1950.

Welter, Allan. *Life in God's Love*. Franciscan Herald Press, 1958.

5. FORMATION; VOCATION

Cegielka, Francis. *Spiritual Theology for Novices*. Immaculate Conception College, 1961.

Cita-Malard, Suzanne. *Religious Orders of Women*. 20th Century Encyclopedia. Hawthorn Books, 1964.

Farrell, Ambrose. *The Education of the Novice*. Newman Press, 1956.

Gambari, Elio. *The Religious Adult in Christ. Religious Formation before Perpetual Profession*. Juniorate Years of Studies. St. Paul's Editions, 1971.

Gambari, Elio. *Religious Apostolic Formation for Sisters*. Fordham, 1964.

Gambari, Elio. *The Updating of Religious Formation.* Text and Commentary on "Instruction on the Renewal of Religious Formation," January 6, 1969. St. Paul's Editions, 1969.

Kohler, Sr. M. Hortense. *Rooted in Hope.* Milwaukee: Bruce, 1962.

Lesage, Germain. *Personalism and Vocation.* Alba House, 1966.

McElhone, James F. *Spirituality for Postulate, Novitiate and Scholasticate.* Ave Maria Press, 1955.

McGoldrick, Desmond. *Holy Restraint. Simple Talks to Sister Novices on the Formation of Religious Personality.* Pittsburgh, 1962.

McGoldrick, Desmond. *The Martyrdom of Change. Simple talks to Postulant Sisters on the Religious Mentality and Ideal.* Pittsburgh, 1961.

Meyers, Bertrande. *The Education of Sisters. A Plan for Integrating the Religious, Cultural, Social and Professional Training of Sisters.* Sheed, 1941.

Molinari, Paul. "Formation to the Religious Life," *The Way,* Supplement. Summer, 1981.

National Catholic Educational Association. Sister Formation Conference. *Report of Everett Curriculum Workshop.* June 1 - August 30, 1956.

O'Keefe, Maureen. *The Convent in the Modern World. A Philosophy of Conventual Living.* Regnery, 1963.

Poage, G. and Germain Lievin (editors). *Today's Vocation Crisis.* A Summary of the Studies and Discussion at the First International Congress on Vocations to the States of Perfection. December 10-16, 1961.

Religious Life Series. *A Manual for Novice Mistresses.* Newman Press, 1957.

Religious Life Series. *Vocation.* Newman Press, 1952.

Ritamary, Sister (ed.) *The Juniorate in Sister Formation.* Proceedings and Communications from Regional Meetings of the Sister Formation Conferences, 1957-1958. Fordham University Press, 1960.

Ritamary, Sister (ed.) *The Mind of the Church in the Formation of Sisters.* New York: Fordham University Press, 1956.

Ritamary, Sister (ed.) *Planning for the Formation of Sisters.* New York: Fordham University Press, 1958.

Ritamary, Sister (ed.). *Spiritual and Intellectual Elements in the Formation of Sisters.* New York: Fordham University Press, 1957.

Schleck, Charles. *The Theology of Vocations.* Milwaukee: Bruce, 1963.

Sikora, Joseph. *Calling. A Reappraisal of Religious Life.* New York: Herder and Herder, 1968.

Sister Formation Conference. *Bulletin.* Official Publication of the Sister Formation Conference. October 1954-Summer, 1958. Milwaukee: Marquette University Press, 1959.

Sister Formation Conference. *Bulletin.* October 1958-Summer, 1962. Milwaukee: Marquette University Press, 1963.

Sister Formation Conference. *Bulletin.* October 1962-Summer 1964. St. Paul: North Central Publishing Company.

Theological Institute for Local Superiors. *The Novitiate.* University of Notre Dame Press, 1961.

Voillaume, Rene. *Follow Me: The Call to Religious Life.* Our Sunday Visitor, 1978.

6. APOSTOLATE

Breckel, Suzanne. *Women in Ministry: A Sister's View.* National Assembly of Women Religious, 1972.

Consortium Perfectae Caritatis. *The Religious Woman, Minister of Faith.* Addresses at first international assembly. February-March, 1974. Boston: St. Paul's, 1974.

Donnelly, Gertrude Joseph. *The Sister Apostle.* Notre Dame Press, 1964.

Images of Women in Mission: A Resource Guide and National Directory of Catholic Church Vocations for Women. Paulist Press, 1981.

Jewett, Paul. *The Ordination of Women.* Grand Rapids: Eerdmann Press, 1980.

Joseph, Mary Vincentia. *New Ministries of Women Religious: Role Conflict and Coping Styles.* Washington, D.C.: Religious Formation Conferences, 1980.

Kenrick, Edward F. *The Spirituality of a Teaching Sister.* St. Louis: Herder, 1962.

Leadership Conference of Women Religious. *New Visions, New Roles: Women in the Church.* Washington, 1975.

Leadership Conference of Women Religious. *Women and Ministry: Present Experience and Future Hopes.* Proceedings of the Symposium based on Women and Ministry: A Survey of the Experience of Roman Catholic Women in the United States. Edited by Doris Gottemoeller and Rita Hofbauer. Washington, D.C., 1981.

Leclercq, Jacques. *The Apostolic Spirituality of the Nursing Sister.* Alba House, 1966.

Ludlow, John. *Woman's Work in the Church.* Historical Notes on Deaconesses and Sisterhoods. Zenger, 1978.

Mary Frederick, Sister. *The Emptying Empire. Religious Women in the Catholic Schools.* Ohio: National Catholic Educational Association, 1969.

Nelson, Joseph. *The Sisterhood and the Apostolate.* Three Conferences at the Institute of Spirituality for Religious Women, 1958. Philadelphia: P. Reilley, 1959.

Religious Life Series. *Apostolic Life*. Newman Press, 1958.

Stuhlmueller, Carroll. *Women and Priesthood. Future Directions.* Collegeville: The Liturgical Press, 1978.

Traxler, Sr. Mary Peter, ed. *New Works for New Nuns*. St. Louis: Herder, 1968.

7. STUDIES IN PSYCHOLOGY AND RELIGIOUS LIFE

Arnold, Magda, et al. *Screening Candidates for the Priesthood and Religious Life*. Chicago: Loyola University Press, 1962.

Canadian Religious Conference. *Psychological Realities and Religious Life*. Ottawa, 1969.

Coville, Walter, *et al. Assessment of Candidates for the Religious Life*. Basic Psychological Issues and Procedures. Center For Applied Research, 1968.

Curran, Charles. *Psychological Dynamics in Religious Living*. New York: Herder and Herder, 1971.

Dondero, E. Austin. *No Borrowed Light. Mental Health For Religious*. Milwaukee: Bruce, 1965.

Evoy, John J. and Van F. Christoph. *Maturity in the Religious Life*. Sheed and Ward, 1965.

Evoy, John J. and Van F. Christoph. *Personality Development in the Religious Life*. Sheed and Ward, 1963.

Evoy, John J. and Van F. Christoph. *The Real Woman in Religious Life*. Sheed and Ward, 1967.

Fichter, Joseph. *Religion as an Occupation. A Study in the Sociology of Professions*. Notre Dame Press, 1961.

Ford, John C. *Religious Superiors, Subjects and Psychiatrists*. Newman Press, 1963.

Franasiak, E. J. ed. *Belonging*. Issues of Emotional Living in an Age of Stress for Clergy and Religious. Affirmation Books, 1978.

Maher, Trafford. *Lest We Build on Sand. Natural Basis for Religious Formation.* St. Louis: Catholic Hospital Association, 1962.

McAllister, Robert. *Conflict in Community.* Institute for Mental Health. Collegeville: St. John's University Press, 1969.

Meissner, William W. *Group Dynamics in the Religious Life.* Notre Dame Press, 1965.

Psychological Symposium. *Coping.* Affirmation Books, 1976.

Psychological Symposium. *Guilt.* Affirmation Books, 1980.

Robinson, Marian Dolores. *Creative Personality in Religious Life.* New York; Sheed and Ward, 1963.

Rulla, L. M. et al. *Psychological Structure and Vocation.* A Study of the Motivations for Entering and Leaving Vocation. Dublin: Villa Books, 1978.

Theological Institute for Local Superiors. *Psychological Dimensions of the Religious Life.* University of Notre Dame Press, 1966.

Van Kaam, Adrian. *Personality Fulfillment in the Religious Life.* Dimension Books, 1967.

Van Kaam, Adrian. *Religion and Personality.* Englewood Cliffs: Prentice-Hall, 1964.

Van Kaam, Adrian. *The Vowed Life: Dynamics of Personal and Spiritual Unfolding.* New Jersey: Dimension Books, 1968.

Weisgerber, Charles. *Psychological Assessment of Candidates for a Religious Order.* Chicago: Loyola University Press, 1969.

8. STUDIES OF RELIGIOUS AND RELIGIOUS ORDERS

Bernstein, Marcelle. *The Nuns.* Philadelphia: Lippincott, 1976.

Campbell-Jones, Suzanne. *In Habit.* A Study of Working Nuns. Pantheon, 1978.

Ebaugh, Helen Rose. *Out of Cloister.* A Study of Organizational Dilemmas. University of Texas Press, 1977.

Ewens, Mary. *The Role of the Nun in the Nineteenth Century.* New York: Arno Press, 1978.

Griffin, Sr. Mary Annarose. *The Courage to Choose. An American Nun's Story.* Little, Brown, 1975.

Harris, Sara. *The Sisters. The Changing World of the American Nun.* New York: Bobbs-Merrill, 1970.

Kinnane, John. *Career Development for Priests and Religious. A Framework for Research and Administration.* Center For Applied Research in the Apostolate, 1970.

Mary Jeremy, Sister. *All The Days of My Life.* 1959.

Mary Vianney, Sister. *And Nora Said Yes.* McMullen, 1953.

Montgomery, Ruth. *Once There Was a Nun. Mary McCarran's Years as Sister Mary Mercy.* Putnam, 1962.

National Sisters Vocation Conference. *A Study on Entrances and Departures in Religious Communities of Women in the United States, 1965-1972.* Conducted by Sister Margaret Modde and Dr. John Koval. Report available in *The Catholic Almanac,* 1974, p. 570.

San Giovanni, Lucinda. *Ex-Nuns. A Study of Emergent Role Passage.* Ablex Publishing Corporation, 1978.

9. DISSERTATIONS ON RELIGIOUS LIFE

Burchill, John P. *Are There Evangelical Counsels of Perpetual Continence and Poverty?* A Study of Tradition. A Reinterpretation of Matthew 19:10-12, 16-22ff, and implications for a Biblical basis of religious life. STD 1975 Dominican House of Studies. 552pp.

Calabro, William V. *Some Organizational Determinants of Orientation to Change: A Case Study of the Attitudes of Women Religious to the Call for "Aggiornamento" in the Catholic Church.* Ph.D. 1976. New York University.

Cortese, Francis. *A Theology of Religious Life According to the Second Vatican Council.* Rome, 1968.

Hammersmith, Sue Kiefer. *Being a Nun: Social Order and Change in a Radical Community.* Ph.D. 1976, Indiana University. 309 pp.

Jancoski, Loretta. *Religion and Commitment: A Psychohistorical Study of Creative Women in Catholic Religious Communities.* Ph.D. 1976. University of Chicago.

McCoskey, Mary Phyllis. *Drastic Social Change of a Closed Community: A Study of a Religious Community That Underwent Change as a Result of Vatican II.* Ph.D. 1976. Bryn Mawr College.

McDermott, Maria Concepta. *A History of Teacher Education in a Congregation of Religious Women.* Sisters of the Holy Cross. Thesis. Notre Dame University, 1964.

McGowan, Claire. *Celibacy, Sexuality, and Meaning in Life.* A Comparative Study of Religious and Catholic Lay Women. Ph.D. 1977. Boston College. 172 pp.

Modde, Margaret Mary. *A Canonical Study of the LCWR of the United States of America.* JCD, 1977, Catholic University of America. 260 pp.

O'Brien, Adrienne. *The Dynamics of Organizational Behavior in Communities of Religious Women.* Ph.D. 1977, Syracuse University. 155pp.

Springstead, Mary Therese. *Problems of Postulants and Novices in Selected Communities of Religious Women.* Ph.D. Fordham University. 223 pp.

SELECTED PERIODICAL LITERATURE

Arbuckle, Gerald A., "Why They Leave: Reflections of a Religious Anthropologist," *Review for Religious* Vol. 42 (1983) No. 6.

Aschenbrenner, George, "Assessing and Choosing Even As the Journey Continues," *Review for Religious*, Vol. 43 (1984) No. 1.

Aschenbrenner, George, "Currents in Spirituality: The Past Decades," *Review for Religious*, Vol. 39 (1980), No. 2.

Aschenbrenner, George, "A God for A Dark Journey: Trends and Issues in Spirituality, 1983," *Review for Religious*, Vol. 42 (1983), No. 2.

Aschenbrenner, George, "Trends and Issues in a Secularizing World," *Review for Religious*, Vol. 41 (1982), No. 6.

Aschenbrenner, George, "Trends in 1980: Some Themes and a Few Specifics," *Review for Religious*, Vol. 40 (1981), No. 2.

Ashley, Benedict, "Self-Study As Instrument of Renewal," *Review for Religious*, Vol. 26 (1967), No. 6.

Brennan, Laetitia, "Ordination of Women: The Cultural Context," *Review for Religious*, Vol. 35 (1976), No. 4.

Casey, Sr. Catherine, "A Selective Bibliography on the Psychology of Sisters," *Review for Religious*, Vol. 36 (1977), No. 2.

Danielou, Jean, "The Place of Religious in the Structure of the Church," *Review for Religious*, Vol. 24 (1965), No. 4.

Davis, Joseph, "Reflections on the Call for Solidarity with the Poor," *Review for Religious*, Vol. 38 (1979), No. 1.

Denis, Sr. Mary, "New Trends in Community Living," *Review for Religious*, Vol. 27 (1968), No. 5.

Dubay, Thomas, "Changing Customs and Religious Obedience," *Review for Religious*, Vol. 32 (1973), No. 2.

Editors, "The Congress of Religious," *Review for Religious*, Vol. 11 (1952).

Emmanuel, Sr. Marie, "Grassroots Sisters Today: Calvary People? Anawim?" *Review for Religious*, Vol. 36 (1977), No. 3.

Faricy, Robert, "Change in the Apostolic Religious Life," *Review for Religious*, Vol. 34 (1975), No. 3.

Ford, John T. "Individual Apostolates and Pluralism in Community Identity," *Review for Religious*, Vol. 35 (1976), No. 6.

Galilea, Segundo, "The Prophetic Challenge of the American Sisters," *Review for Religious*, Vol. 32 (1973), No. 1.

Gottemoeller, Sr. Doris, "Religious Government: A Reflection on Relationships," *Review for Religious*, Vol. 34 (1975), No. 3.

Hallow, Sr. Mary Kevin, "Development of a Constitution," *Review for Religious*, Vol. 41 (1981), No. 6.

Isabell, Damien and Brother Joachim, "Bibliography for Renewal," *Review for Religious*, Vol. 26 (1967), No. 1.

Jegen, Sr. Mary Evelyn, "Religious and Social Justice," *Review for Religious*, Vol. 38 (1979), No. 2.

Johnson, Elizabeth A. "Discipleship: Root Model of the Life Called 'Religious'" *Review for Religious*, Vol. 42 (1983), No. 6.

Joseph, Sr. Mary Vincentia and Sr. Carla Przybilla, "Preparation for New Ministries: A Futuristic View," *Review for Religious*, Vol. 30 (1977), No. 6.

Kosicki, George, "Assume Nothing: On Making Assumptions Explicit in Religious Renewal," *Review for Religious*, Vol. 36 (1977), No. 5.

Kosicki, George, "Renewed Religious Life; The Dynamics of Re-discovery," *Review for Religious*, Vol. 35, (1976), No. 1.

Larkin, Ernest, "The Scriptural-Theological Aspects of Religious Life," *Review for Religious*, Vol. 27 (1968), No. 6.

Latkovich, Sallie, "On Choosing Religious Life Today," *Review for Religious*, Vol. 43 (1984) No. 3.

LaVerdiere, Eugene, "Renewal of Religious Life in Historical Perspective," *Review for Religious*, Vol. 26 (1967), No. 6.

Lescher, Bruce, "Toward a Spirituality of Liminality," *Review for Religious*, Vol. 39 (1980), No. 5.

Lozano, Juan M. "The Revision of the Constitution: Meaning, Criteria and Problems," *Review for Religious*, Vol. 34 (1975), No. 4.

McDermott, Sr. Rose of Lima, "Governance in Religious Life," *Review for Religious*, Vol. 39 (1980), No. 3.

Miller, Sr. Jo Ann, "The Future of Religious Life is Now," *Review for Religious*, Vol. 40 (1981), No. 4.

Neal, Sr. Marie Augusta, "The Relationship Between Religious Belief and Structural Change in Religious Orders: Part I: Developing an Effective Measuring Instrument,"

Review of Religious Research, Vol. 11 (1970); "Part II: Some Evidence," *Review of Religious Research*, Vol. 12 (1971).

Neal, Sr. Marie Augusta, "The Sisters' Survey, 1980: A Report," *Probe*. National Association of Women Religious, Vol. 10 (May-June, 1981). No. 5.

O'Connor John, "The Meaning of History and the Renewal of Religious Life," *Review for Religious*, Vol. 28 (1969), No. 3.

Oliva, Max, "Integration of Faith and Justice: Spiritual Renewal for Our Times," *Review for Religious*, Vol. 41 (1982), No. 2.

Page, Thomas M., "Managing and Planning Changes in Religious Institutes," *Review for Religious*, Vol. 31 (1972), No. 3.

Quinn, John, "The Pastoral Service of Bishops to Religious," *Review for Religious*, Vol. 43 (1984), No. 2.

Quinn, John R. "Religious Life: The Mystery and the Challenge," *Review for Religious*, Vol. 42 (1983) No. 6.

Ribando, William R., "Religious and the Coming Crisis in Ministry," *Review for Religious*, Vol. 35 (1976), No. 5.

Ringkamp, Henry, "Pre-retirement and Retirement Programs for Religious," *Review for Religious*, Vol. 35 (1976), No. 2.

Rosato, Philip, "Towards a Vision of Religious Life," *Review for Religious*, Vol. 36 (1977), No. 4.

Richardine, Sister Mary, "The Evolution of the Idea of Sister Formation, 1952-1960," *Sponsa Regis*, Vol. 33 (April, 1962), No. 8.

Said, Mark, "Particular Law of Institutes in the Renewal of Consecrated Life," *Review for Religious*, Vol. 36 (1977), No. 6.

Scarpino, Sr. Georgine, "Beyond Consensus: The Role of Assumptional Analysis in Congregational Decision-Making," *Review for Religious*, Vol. 41 (1982), No. 1.

Sheets, John, "The Call to the Renewal of Religious Life," *Review for Religious* Vol. 43 (1984), No. 2.

Sheets, John, "Soundings on the Present State of Religious Life," *Review for Religious*, Vol. 31 (1972), No. 3.

Wenzel, Sr. Kristin, "Towards a Sociology of Ministry in the United States," *Review for Religious*, Vol. 41 (1982), No. 4.

Wittberg, Patricia, "Sociology and Religious Life: Call for a New Integration," *Review for Religious*, Vol. 42 (1983), No. 6.